Praise for **What to Do When You Have a Tricky, Sticky, Picky Brain**

"*What to Do When You Have a Tricky, Sticky, Picky Brain* is the most comprehensive and engaging resource I've seen for helping kids understand and manage OCD. Dr. Jacob translates proven treatments into language and strategies that truly connect with children and families. This book is not only based on the latest research, but it is compassionate, empowering, and truly an indispensable guide for kids learning to take charge of their OCD and live fully."

—Jonathan Abramowitz, PhD, professor of psychology at the University of North Carolina at Chapel Hill and author of *The Family Guide to Getting Over OCD*

"In this appealing and highly readable book, Dr. Jacob brings hope and optimism to young people with OCD. She artfully portrays the ins and outs of OCD and the concepts of effective cognitive behavioral therapy, bringing clarity to complexity. The abundance of relatable examples, illustrations, callouts, and worksheets makes it an excellent practical guide for any youth to navigate OCD. I recommend it wholeheartedly!"

—Aureen P. Wagner, PhD, the Anxiety Wellness Center, author of *Up and Down the Worry Hill* and *What to Do When Your Child Has OCD*

"*What to Do When You Have a Tricky, Sticky, Picky Brain* is the book I wish our therapist had when my young daughter first needed help for OCD. Dr. Marni Jacob translates complex symptoms and treatment strategies into language kids can understand—while giving clinicians and families a shared roadmap for navigating care together. As a past president of the International OCD Foundation who has decades of experience in advocacy for kids, I know how urgently a resource like this is needed. Its breadth, depth, and kid-friendly clarity make it a standout companion guide for pediatric OCD treatment."

—Susan Boaz, past president of the International OCD Foundation and executive director of the PANDAS Physicians Network

"This book is a gem! I predict it will be a classic must-read for anyone dealing with pediatric OCD, whether personally, as a parent, or as a clinician. Dr. Jacob shares her clinical brilliance with practical and attention-grabbing pearls of wisdom for the field. She speaks directly to children and youth with OCD, giving them the straight facts while inspiring hope and self-efficacy. Introducing characters such as 'Just-Right Juan,' 'Magical Thinking Mila,' and 'Need-to-Know Nancy,' this book helps readers recognize the many faces of OCD—and will undoubtedly make those affected by this condition feel more understood."

—Evelyn Stewart, MD, FRCPC, director of the BC Children's Hospital OCD program, professor of psychiatry at the University of British Columbia, and coauthor of *OCD in Children and Adolescents: The "OCD Is Not the Boss of Me" Manual*

"As a parent who has walked alongside a child with OCD, I'm grateful for a resource that speaks to kids with clarity, compassion, and real clinical insight. *What to Do When You Have a Tricky, Sticky, Picky Brain* helps demystify OCD and equip kids with practical, evidence-based tools they can use—while helping them feel seen rather than alone. This is a resource I'd recommended to every family navigating OCD; it's the guide I wish my daughter had."

—Chris Baier, parent of a teen with OCD and producer of *Unstuck: An OCD Kids Movie*

"*What to Do When You Have a Tricky, Sticky, Picky Brain* may just be the most comprehensive book written for OCD that I have ever seen, and I have a bookshelf full of books on OCD!

Dr. Jacob serves you the entire spread of OCD—it is an A to Z and back again manual that is engaging and inspirational for all kids, and their caregivers too. This is a must-read for families who are dealing with OCD."

—**Patrick B. McGrath, PhD,** chief clinical officer of NOCD

"*What to Do When You Have a Tricky, Sticky, Picky Brain* is the book I wish every family and clinician had when a child is diagnosed with OCD. Its explanations of ERP are practical and incredibly accessible, offering strategies kids can actually use. In my work with youth experiencing religious OCD, I have long needed a resource that speaks to the full range of OCD presentations with clarity and compassion, and this book finally fills that gap. Its comprehensive scope and ability to normalize even the trickiest OCD themes make it a must-have in every OCD toolbox."

—**Rev. Katie O'Dunne, DMin,** founder and director of Stick with the Ick, an inclusive community app supporting individuals with OCD, clinicians, and clergy navigating faith and scrupulosity

"OCD in kids often flies under the radar; it doesn't always look like counting and cleaning. But when it's recognized early, kids can make huge progress because their brains are still wonderfully bendy. *What to Do When You Have a Tricky, Sticky, Picky Brain* turns tricky science into teachable skills and tools that can have a profound impact on kids struggling with OCD. It's a game-changer for classrooms and clinics alike."

—**Ethan Smith,** CEO, former IOCDF national advocate, and executive producer of *Waving* and *Uncovering OCD: The Truth About Obsessive Compulsive Disorder*

"I've worked with kids who have OCD for over 20 years, and I wish that I could have given them all this book! Dr. Jacob lays out not just what OCD looks like and how tricky it can be, but also how to fight back against it in the most effective way possible. This book will be at the top of my recommendations for kids with OCD and their parents, as a great resource both on its own and when working with an OCD specialist."

—**Caleb W. Lack, PhD,** professor of psychology at the University of Central Oklahoma and faculty member of the International OCD Foundation

"This is a practical step-by-step book to help children and adolescents understand, challenge, and overcome OCD. The chapters are easy to read, include structured activities to guide implementing strategies, and conclude with a helpful, succinct summary. The visual graphics and patient quotes convey complex therapeutic concepts in an easy-to-understand manner. This is a must-have resource for any young person dealing with OCD."

—**Joseph McGuire, PhD,** professor of psychiatry and behavioral sciences and director of research in the Division of Child and Adolescent Psychiatry at Johns Hopkins University School of Medicine

"Dr. Jacob has done a massive service to kids and teens with OCD and their families by writing a fun, informative, and effective book on how to beat a tricky, sticky, picky brain. This book is one of the first written directly for children and teens that provides them with practical yet effective strategies for understanding and, most importantly, taking control over their OCD."

—**Eric Storch, PhD,** McIngvale Presidential Endowed Chair and professor at Baylor College of Medicine

What to Do When You Have a

Tricky, Sticky, Picky Brain

Cognitive Behavioral Strategies to **Help Kids** with **Obsessive-Compulsive Disorder**

By Marni L. Jacob, PHD, ABPP

WHAT TO DO WHEN YOU HAVE A TRICKY, STICKY, PICKY BRAIN

Published by
PESI Publishing, Inc.
3839 White Ave
Eau Claire, WI 54703

Cover and interior design by Emily Dyer
Editing by Jenessa Jackson, PhD

ISBN 9781683738886 (print)
ISBN 9781683738893 (ePUB)
ISBN 9781683738909 (ePDF)

Printed in the United States of America.

Dedication

To Emma and Mason, the greatest joy of all is being your mother.
May you always believe in yourself and follow your dreams.
I love you more than anything.

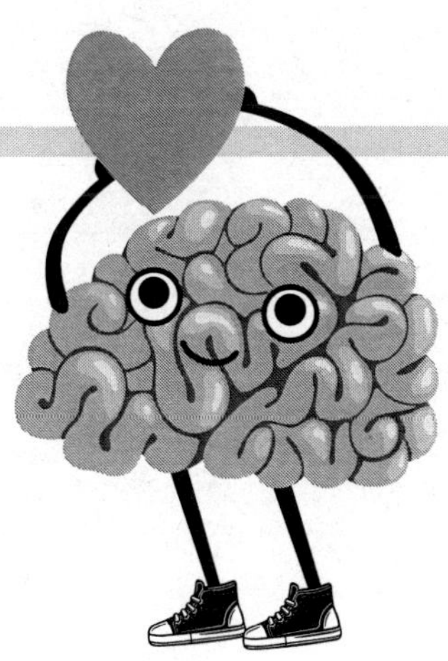

Table of Contents

Foreword

Okay, here's the deal. If you're reading this, it probably means that you have something called *obsessive-compulsive disorder* (OCD). It might sound a little intimidating, but don't sweat it *too*, too much. This is an incredibly common condition that affects about 2 percent of children and adolescents at any given point. That means if you are going to summer camp with 100 other kids, roughly 2 of them will have OCD. On top of that, a whole bunch more of these kids are likely to have upsetting thoughts or repetitive behaviors that get in the way but don't quite meet the classification of OCD. The bottom line is that you are among a very large group of individuals in the world who struggle with this condition.

Let's go with the assumption that you have OCD. The next question to ask yourself is what are you going to do about it? To me—someone who has worked for twenty-five years in helping children and adults with OCD—one of the biggest factors that comes into play in beating OCD is through hard work in applying tried-and-true principles of a therapy called *cognitive behavioral therapy* (CBT). This treatment has been tested in many studies in kids with OCD all around the world. And I am happy to share with you that every single study shows CBT to be extremely effective; not only is it helpful in gaining control over OCD, but it remains helpful for a very long time when you keep using the skills that you have learned. In fact, one recent study found that more than 90 percent of children and teens were doing extremely well three years after getting therapy for their OCD. And after having done this work for over twenty years (yes, that means I'm old!), I know that kids continue to do great when they keep practicing the tools they've learned to fight back against OCD. This means that there is great hope that you can take charge of your OCD and do all the things you want to do in your life. It's just going to take a little bit of hard work to do so, but hey, it's much harder to have OCD than it is to do the work in order to beat it.

As you're reading this, you might be thinking, "This guy seems pretty cool and sounds like he knows his stuff." But here's the truth: I am quite the nerd (a cool nerd?). I am the type of guy who wakes up early in the morning before everyone else so I can work on a research paper that explains a scientific discovery to help people with OCD. I love it. It is my life's passion, and I am so proud of all the work that we have done so far to support kids just like you. However, there is one thing that has been missing from the field of OCD, but I can tell you—quite happily—that we have finally addressed it with the book that you are about to read.

Before sharing what it is, I want to tell you a little story. One day, about twenty years or so ago, I was giving a guest lecture in a clinical psychology class at the University of Florida. When I finished speaking, a very energetic and confident young student introduced herself to me and said, "I want to work in your lab and do research to help kids." Now, this isn't the first time that's happened. But there was something very impressive about this person, especially her confidence and her passion to learn more about helping people who are struggling. That individual not only worked in my lab as a college student, but soon after, she became my first-ever research coordinator, and after getting her PhD in clinical psychology, she came back to complete several additional years of training with me. Now, that goal she had to help kids was even stronger and had become laser-focused on OCD. By now, you can probably guess who I'm talking about: the author of this very book, Dr. Marni Jacob.

Dr. Jacob identified the major gap in the field that I was talking about earlier—there had not yet existed a comprehensive, up-to-date, and well-tailored book designed to help kids and teens with their OCD. But we are happy to report that the book you are holding in front of you is exactly that. There are so many qualities about this book that make it the perfect tool to help kids like you who might be struggling with this condition. Still need convincing? Here are a few reasons why this book can help you.

First, let's keep it real. I know it can be hard to read stuff, especially when it is about something as difficult and personal as OCD. This disorder is also often misunderstood by people because there are so many different ways it can show up. But Dr. Jacob does an amazing job of explaining information to you through a variety of characters that cover pretty much every way OCD can present. She dives into the many ways that OCD appears—way more than other books I've seen—so you can recognize yourself in the characters as you plan your strategy for fighting back. She also discusses lots of "tricks" and "traps" that OCD likes to use to keep you stuck, and more importantly, how to understand them in order to break free from OCD's grip.

Second, I'm the type of guy who likes to browse the psychology section in bookstores. Okay, it sounds a little nerdy, but when I look at all the books there, I see a lot of different information, and I'll be honest with you—a lot of the stuff that gets published isn't based on informed science and what we know about how best to address OCD. That is absolutely not the case in this book. Each and every component discussed here is based on well-researched and proven approaches. In particular, the core element of this book, facing your fears, is based in CBT, which has helped so many kids just like you. One of the most powerful ways to gain control over your OCD is by facing your fears using a very powerful tool called *exposure and response prevention* (ERP). What's cool is that you can even do this on your own (although sometimes having a therapist partner with you and your family can be a big help!). Dr. Jacob explains this in a way that makes it easy to understand and even easier to put into action. She helps you see how OCD tricks you into doing *compulsions*—actions or mental rituals that might feel like they bring relief but actually make OCD stronger. She also shows you how to break free from OCD's grip by facing your fears in small manageable steps, giving you the tools to become stronger each time you practice.

Third, while learning how to face your fears is a key part of the book, what makes this book stand out is the way Dr. Jacob covers OCD's many nuances—every twist, every turn, and every trick it might try to play. She doesn't just give you general advice; she gets specific, helping you understand your own OCD and how to fight back in a way that works for you. She reviews "thinking traps" to look out for, how to keep up your motivation to fight back against OCD, and how to address anything that might get in the way. There are very few kids' books that talk about this stuff, and such knowledge will really boost your success.

Fourth, and finally, this book explores the unique pressures and challenges that come with being a child or adolescent with OCD—whether it's school stress, social media, family dynamics, or just trying to figure out who you are and what is important to you. OCD doesn't stop because you're busy, and it can make everything feel a lot harder than it needs to be. But with the strategies in this book, you can learn to manage OCD while still living your very best life.

To wrap things up, let me start by saying I am so happy that you have this book in your hands. But the next step is yours. Remember, you don't have to face OCD alone. This book provides the guidance and support you need to start your journey toward healing. With time, practice, and the right tools, you can take control of OCD and live the life you want to live—free from OCD's hold. So, take a deep breath, and know that every page you turn brings you one step closer to mastering your OCD. You've got this because OCD isn't in charge. You are. You're stronger than OCD, and with the knowledge and skills in these pages, you'll soon see just how powerful you really are.

Eric A. Storch, PhD
McIngvale Presidential Endowed Chair and Professor
Vice Chair and Head of Psychology
Menninger Department of Psychiatry and Behavioral Sciences
Baylor College of Medicine

A Note to Parents and Caregivers

If you have purchased this book for a child in your life, I want to start by saying thank you. Thank you for helping your child see that they are not alone and that they can learn strategies to ensure that OCD doesn't control their life.

Statistics show that it often takes many years before people get an accurate diagnosis of OCD—and even more years before people get effective treatment. By sharing this resource with your child now, I hope it will help us start to turn those statistics around.

I wrote this book for a variety of reasons. First, I found that most kids with OCD really want to know more about what they are struggling with. I therefore wanted to write something for kids that went into detail about the types of questions that often come up, which can help them take ownership in tackling this tough but very treatable disorder.

Second, I wanted to write a book that was as comprehensive as possible in discussing the breadth and depth of how OCD can manifest. For that reason, this book discusses a wide array of common OCD symptoms, beyond just the stereotypical presentations that are often talked about. This includes excessive concerns about morality or religion, intrusive or taboo thoughts, and many lesser-known presentations of OCD, which occur far more commonly in youth than most people realize. It was important to me to include these OCD symptoms so I could reach *all* the kids who suffer in silence with these often-misunderstood concerns. Though I discuss these symptoms in developmentally appropriate ways, I encourage you to review the book first if you have any hesitations about how I might discuss the various themes in OCD.

Third, and similarly, I really wanted to write a book that normalized the doubts and challenges that often come with OCD so I could destigmatize the disorder and help kids see that they are not alone. By pairing that with my fourth (and final) goal of providing evidence-based strategies to help kids gain control of OCD, I hope this book will make a difference in your child's life!

Sincerely,
Marni L. Jacob, PhD, ABPP

Introduction

Hey! What's up? It's great to meet you! I hear you have a *tricky*, *sticky*, *picky* brain—also known as obsessive-compulsive disorder (OCD)—just like me! For so long, I thought I was the only one. I didn't think anyone understood what I was going through. I felt odd, different, and weird. There were times when I didn't feel like myself at all. It was really difficult because I didn't know who to talk to or what to do. Have you ever felt like that?

I later realized that there are tons of kids, teens, and even adults *just like us.* In fact, I learned that about 1 to 2 out of every 100 kids have similar struggles. That means if there are more than 100 kids in your school, there's a good chance a couple of them have a *tricky*, *sticky*, *picky* brain too. And if you think about how many other schools there are across the world, that's a ton of kids just like you! If you're in a movie theater or mall, at an amusement park, or on an airplane, I bet a few people there have one too. There are people all over the world with *tricky*, *sticky*, *picky* brains—you may just not know many of them since it's typically not obvious who has one and who doesn't.

Since I realized that it's pretty common to have a *tricky*, *sticky*, *picky* brain, I've been on a journey to learn a lot about it, including what to do when it makes me feel worried, scared, or upset. I've learned that it isn't my fault that my brain works this way, and I am able to do something about it. By sharing what I've learned, I hope that you will be inspired to start using these same skills so that you can learn to challenge your *tricky*, *sticky*, *picky* brain too!

Throughout my journey, I've also made a lot of friends who have *tricky*, *sticky*, *picky* brains. For instance, there's Doubting Danny, Perfectionistic Pete, Need-to-Know Nancy, Organizing Oscar, "Just-Right" Juan, Scary-Thought Susie, Moral Marcus, Contamination-Concerned Charlie, Magical Thinking Mila, Superstitious Solomon, Religious Ryder, and many others. There are so many people just like us. In chapter 12, I will introduce you to them all, and each of them will share a bit about what they did to overcome their *tricky*, *sticky*, *picky* brains. I'll also discuss how you can build the motivation to fight back against OCD, lean on your family for help, and develop strategies to stop it from interfering with school, friends, and so much more. So, let's get to it! I'll start by telling you a little more about what I've learned about my *tricky*, *sticky*, *picky* brain . . .

CHAPTER 1

What I've Learned About My *Tricky, Sticky, Picky* Brain

Ever since I realized that I have a *tricky*, *sticky*, *picky* brain, I've learned a lot about how my brain works. It's *tricky* in that it tries to convince or "trick" me into believing that certain things are true when they aren't. It's *sticky* in that there are thoughts that seem to get "stuck" in my head, and no matter how hard I try, it's difficult to get them to stop bothering me. It's *picky* in that it's very specific in terms of what it wants, and it often pesters me until things are a very particular way.

I've learned that there isn't anything wrong with me; it's just that my brain works a little differently than others. When someone has OCD, their brain tends to get stuck on bothersome thoughts, images, or urges that often cause anxiety or other unpleasant emotions. These sticky thoughts, which are known as *obsessions*, keep coming back over and over again, but the person can't stop thinking about them. Obsessions can be worrisome, upsetting, scary, or annoying. For example, someone may have obsessions about being "contaminated," leading them to obsess over germs, dirt, and cleanliness. Or they might have obsessions about being moral, so they'll worry about always doing the "right" thing.

Further, people with a *tricky, sticky, picky* brain tend to engage in certain behaviors or rituals to feel better. For example, someone with obsessions about germs and cleanliness may wash their hands repeatedly or sterilize things in an attempt to decrease anxiety about being "contaminated." Or someone with obsessions about morality might seek reassurance from others about whether they did something wrong. These behaviors are known as *compulsions*, and they are *tricky* in that they actually have the opposite effect and make things worse. Throughout this book, I'll discuss how to stop giving in to compulsions and replace them with real strategies that will help you feel better.

Obsessions: Unwanted thoughts, images, or urges that keep popping into your mind and that cause anxiety, distress, or other unpleasant emotions

Compulsions: Ritualistic or repetitive behaviors (can be physical or mental) that you feel like you *have* to do to reduce the anxiety or distress that is often associated with obsessions

Obsessive-compulsive disorder: When obsessions (thoughts, images, urges) and compulsions (rituals, repetitive behaviors) are significant enough to cause a lot of distress and get in the way of your day-to-day life

I've also learned that people with a *tricky, sticky, picky* brain tend to think about things in unhelpful or flawed ways. For instance, they tend to fall into certain thinking traps, which are skewed ways of thinking that cause you to feel worried or upset. Once you can recognize these thinking traps, you will be less likely to fall for them. I'll mention several of them in chapter 4 so you can get into the habit of spotting these traps in your own thinking.

At this point, I bet you're wondering *why* all this happens, so let's start by going over some of the reasons why doctors think that some people have a *tricky, sticky, picky* brain.

What Causes a *Tricky, Sticky, Picky* Brain?

Once I realized I had a *tricky, sticky, picky* brain, I was on a quest to figure out why! I wanted to know what caused my brain to think this way and why some people are like this but others aren't. In doing so, I learned that there isn't one clear-cut reason for what causes a *tricky, sticky, picky* brain, but here is some of what researchers have discovered so far.

Differences in Brain Function

Scientists have found some differences in how certain brain systems work in people with OCD. There is a communication loop in the brain that sends messages between the deeper parts of the brain that handle instincts and emotions (called the *subcortex*) with the parts at the front and outside of the brain that handle thinking, planning, and controlling behavior (called the *prefrontal cortex*). This messaging circuit is called the *cortico-striato-thalamico-cortical circuit*, and it is overactive in OCD, especially in regions that monitor for errors or potential threats. Don't worry about remembering these fancy brain names—in fact, let's just call this one "the communication circuit" for short!

When the communication circuit is overactive, the brain may keep sending "something is wrong" messages in situations that aren't really so dangerous. It's as if alarms and sirens are going off to warn us about something scary when there really isn't anything to be scared of. Or if something is a little scary, this overactive circuit makes us think it's much more scary or risky than it actually is. It's a bit like having a smoke detector that's overly sensitive. It still works, but it goes off too easily and has trouble calming down once it has been set off.

This same overactive circuit can also cause us to have a bias toward more worrisome or threatening thoughts, compared to more neutral thoughts. Consider the following sentence: "The doctor measured Ana's growth." What do you first think when you read that? Some people might interpret "growth" to mean a cancerous tumor, while others might interpret "growth" to reference Ana's height. When the communication circuit is overactive, we're more likely to interpret something vague and neutral (like the sentence about Ana) as dangerous or threatening, when that may not necessarily be the case.

People with OCD also show variations in the activity levels in other parts of the brain, including the part of the brain that is involved in habit formation and controlling movement (known as the *basal ganglia*) and a part that controls emotional responses and decision-making (known as the *orbitofrontal cortex*). The point is, if we looked at what was going on inside the brain of someone with OCD and compared it to someone without OCD, we'd likely see that certain areas are more active in OCD. The *tricky, sticky, picky* brain would look more lit up (like bright fireworks going off) while the non–*tricky, sticky, picky* brain would be much calmer.

Although people with OCD have these differences in brain functioning, it doesn't have to stay that way! With the right tools (like the skills in this book), you can actually retrain your *tricky, sticky, picky* brain to respond to these alarm signals differently, so that it functions more like the brain of someone without OCD. How cool is that?

Genetics

Genes are the building blocks of your body. They help make you who you are! For example, genes carry information that determines whether you have blue eyes or brown eyes, and whether you are short or tall. They also play a role in other aspects of who you are, such as whether you are outgoing or shy. Your genes are passed down (or *inherited*) from your birth parents, and *heredity* is the term that scientists use to describe this process. The chance that you will have certain traits (e.g., blue eyes versus brown eyes) depends on specific genes that your parents pass down to you. For example, if both of your parents have brown eyes, you will have a greater chance of having brown eyes than if neither parent has brown eyes.

Just as genes help determine our eye and hair color, they also play a role in OCD. In fact, children of a parent with OCD are 25 percent more likely to have OCD. That means it's more likely that someone will have OCD if they have family members who also have OCD. Researchers have learned a lot about this by conducting studies on twins and comparing the heritability of OCD in identical twins compared to fraternal twins. Some of this research is even trying to identify whether there may be specific genes linked to OCD, but a lot more work is needed in this area.

Neurotransmitters

Our brains have chemical messengers called *neurotransmitters* that carry messages throughout the brain. If you think of your brain as a city, the neurotransmitters would act as postal workers that deliver information to allow the city to run smoothly. When one part of the city (or brain) wants to talk to another part, neurotransmitters help with this communication. It is suspected that people with OCD have different levels of certain neurotransmitters in their brain, which impacts how their brain functions. For example, in people with OCD, there is a specific type of neurotransmitter (known as *serotonin*) that is absorbed too quickly without having enough time to deliver all the messages as part of its job. For that reason, treatment for OCD often involves the use of medication to improve how serotonin functions in the brain.

Here's a silly example to help explain this. Let's imagine that you drop a bunch of candy on the floor that you were planning to eat. A vacuum suddenly comes by and sucks up all the candy before you get the chance to pick it up and eat it. Major bummer! If only you had a little brother to block the vacuum from sucking up the candy, you'd have enough time to devour it all. Now that would be siblings working together! Medications for OCD are thought to act similarly, in that they slow down how quickly serotonin is absorbed so it can hang out in your brain a little longer and do its job.

That was a ridiculous example, but hopefully it gives you an idea of how medications help treat OCD. When these medications work as planned, people find that it is easier to manage their *tricky, sticky, picky* brain so they can stop getting stuck in thinking traps and start doing what matters to them.

Other Factors

Social Influences

Sometimes people develop certain patterns of thinking, feeling, and behaving by watching and learning from others, such as their parents. For example, if you have a parent who works really hard at their soccer game, you may be inspired to learn a soccer skill of your own. That also means if you have a parent who tends to worry a lot or be overly fearful, that may rub off on you too. You may see how they handle certain situations and end up behaving in similar ways. For example, if they freak out every time they see a bug in the house (or if they're stuck in traffic or have a work deadline), then you may react this way too. If they seem shy and hesitant in social situations and that causes them to avoid those situations, you might find yourself acting the same way. These social influences can play a role in how OCD develops and is maintained.

Illnesses, Infections, and Sudden Symptom Presentations

Some kids develop OCD very suddenly, alongside big changes in anxiety, mood, and behavior. Doctors call this type of onset *pediatric acute-onset neuropsychiatric syndrome* (PANS). There are some links to this occurring after exposure to certain illnesses or infections. For example, the development of one specific type of PANS, called *pediatric autoimmune neuropsychiatric disorder associated with streptococcus* (PANDAS), is linked to getting strep throat. To treat OCD that is associated with these types of exposures, doctors may use antibiotics or other medicines that help fight off bacteria, viruses, and infections in addition to the skills discussed in this book.

Stress

Some people start to experience OCD after something really stressful or upsetting happens. Though we don't have evidence to say that stress or trauma *causes* OCD, it is possible that it could trigger OCD to come out. Consider a child who is born with a higher chance of having OCD (due to their genes) but doesn't show symptoms of it until middle or high school. Or consider a child who has some minor symptoms of OCD that fly under the radar for a while and don't really cause much of a problem. Then, a stressful event occurs, like moving to a new home, an experience with a bully, an exciting but important performance, or a death in the family, which triggers their OCD to come out. It's as if they were walking around with a cup filled to the very top with water, and then some rain filled it up even more, causing the water to overflow and make a mess. It's the same with OCD: Stress or trauma can send some kids' symptoms over the edge and cause OCD to "spill out" into the open.

SUMMARY

I know that was a lot of information! All you need to remember is that although there is likely no one single cause of OCD, we do have some pretty good ideas about what factors might be involved, and scientists are continuing to learn more as time goes on. In the next chapter, I'll explain some of the ways that having a *tricky, sticky, picky* brain can affect you—and in later chapters, I'll teach you step-by-step strategies you can use to gain control over OCD so it no longer picks on you in such frustrating and upsetting ways.

CHAPTER 2

Ways Your *Tricky, Sticky, Picky* Brain May Pick on You

Now that we've gone over the basics of what it means to have *a tricky, sticky, picky* brain, we can get into some of the specific ways that it picks on us. I'll start by providing you with brief summaries of several common themes that often occur in OCD, followed by a series of checklists that describe the most common ways OCD can affect people. These checklists don't include *every* single OCD symptom, but they are based on tons of research on people with OCD, which has found that many children, teens, and adults are bothered by the same kinds of things.

Start by reading through several common themes in OCD and pay attention to any concerns that you relate to. Remember, though, that just because you relate to any of these concerns does not necessarily mean that they're based in OCD. That's because it's normal to occasionally worry about making a mistake or something bad happening, or to find yourself going back to check over your homework or to see if you turned off your lights. It's only considered OCD if the thoughts, images, or urges get stuck in your mind (obsessions) or if you feel like you *have* to engage in repetitive or ritualistic behaviors (compulsions) to reduce the anxiety or discomfort caused by the obsessions. These compulsions must also be excessive (i.e., you do them much more than what would be typical or necessary), cause significant distress, or interfere with your ability to function in your day-to-day life.

In addition, keep in mind that while certain OCD symptoms often occur together, the majority of people with *tricky, sticky, picky* brains have symptoms that cut across different themes. For example, someone with OCD might worry about getting contaminated by germs (obsession), which leads to them to repeatedly wash their hands (compulsion). Alternatively, someone else with OCD might feel the need to compulsively wash their hands—*not* because they're afraid of germs, but because they have intrusive thoughts about something bad happening (obsession) and they think that the handwashing (compulsion) will somehow counteract the scary thought. While it might not make sense that handwashing would neutralize a scary thought, remember that OCD is often based in irrational and bizarre thoughts, urges, and behaviors, so obsessions are not always logically connected to compulsions. Essentially, any obsession can be linked with any compulsion and vice versa.

COMMON THEMES IN OCD

Contamination concerns: People with these concerns are excessively preoccupied with being contaminated in some way. They might worry that they (or others) will fall ill as a result of being exposed to germs, or they might be concerned about being unable to tolerate the feeling of being contaminated (e.g., feeling "dirty" or "disgusted"). These concerns often lead them to engage in repetitive cleaning rituals (e.g., excessive washing, showering, or sanitizing) or to avoid objects or situations that trigger these worries (e.g., public bathrooms, dirty shoes).

"Just-right" symptoms: People with these symptoms are driven by a need to do things in a particular way in order to feel "just right." They worry that if they don't make things feel "just right," something bad could happen, or they worry that they'll continue to feel distressed or "off" in some way and will have trouble moving on unless they rid themselves of that feeling. For their compulsions, they might attempt to make things even, symmetrical, or arranged in a particular way. They may also repeatedly count, touch, tap, or say things (either out loud or in their mind) until they feel an internal sense of balance, satisfaction, or completeness.

Checking symptoms: People with these symptoms have the urge to repeatedly check things to resolve feelings of doubt or uncertainty. For example, they may repeatedly check that the door is locked, the stove is turned off, or the hair dryer is unplugged. They may also replay past events in their head to make sure they didn't make a mistake or do something wrong—as if they are essentially "checking" their past actions. They may also check and recheck homework assignments, emails, or text messages. People with checking behaviors may engage in these rituals because they're worried that something bad will happen (e.g., a fire will start because they left the stove on) or that they will make a mistake (e.g., they'll turn in a homework assignment with multiple typos), and the checking serves to reduce or eliminate that risk as well as any associated anxiety or doubt.

Intrusive or "taboo" thoughts: Many people with OCD experience bothersome, unwanted, or taboo thoughts that are often referred to as *intrusive thoughts*. These can include (1) aggressive, scary, or harmful thoughts; (2) thoughts that feel gross, inappropriate, or sexual in nature; or (3) thoughts that go against their religion, faith, or morality. Since these thoughts often make the person feel afraid, confused, disgusted, ashamed, or embarrassed, they will try to cancel out the thoughts, push the thoughts out of their mind, or make up for the thoughts in some way. They may also try to seek reassurance from others or share their thoughts with loved ones so they can be told that they're not a bad person. Finally, they try to avoid situations or people that trigger these thoughts because they're afraid they may act on the thoughts and they want to reduce the risk of harm.

Existential or philosophical concerns: People with these concerns experience obsessions that often focus on "big life" questions, such as "What is the meaning of life?"; "What's my purpose?"; "Why are we here?"; or "What happens after we die?" They may also obsess about the origin of the earth, the massive size of the universe, or what is or isn't "real." People with these OCD symptoms often spend an excessive amount of time researching the meaning of things or seeking reassurance in effort to answer these unanswerable questions.

Now that you've learned about some common themes in OCD, read through the following checklists of OCD symptoms and check off any that you've experienced. Make sure to only check off symptoms that you've experienced *excessively*—meaning it's to the point that it takes up a lot of time or causes problems for you. For example, it's normal to check over your homework assignment before turning it in, but if you find yourself checking over it four, five, six (or more!) times, it's a sign that it might be related to OCD. When I did this myself, I was surprised to see that so many things that I have struggled with are on this list! It helped me realize that I'm really not alone in what I'm going through. My hope is that it will do the same for you. Then, we'll use anything you check off to make a plan to challenge your *tricky, sticky, picky* brain!

FEAR OF GERMS AND CONTAMINATION

- ❒ Worrying about getting germs on yourself and catching an illness or disease
- ❒ Worrying about contaminating or spreading germs to others
- ❒ Washing or cleaning excessively (e.g., washing your hands more than necessary, using a lot of hand sanitizer, taking really long showers, wiping down personal belongings)
- ❒ Spending a lot of time brushing your teeth, using the toilet, or doing things related to personal hygiene

- ❒ Using barriers to avoid contact with germs (e.g., using a paper towel or your shirt to open the door)
- ❒ Worrying about getting contaminated from chemicals or poisonous substances (e.g., household cleaners, pesticides)
- ❒ Being bothered by urine, poop, saliva, blood, or other bodily fluids
- ❒ Being bothered by the *feeling* of being "dirty," "contaminated," or "disgusted"
- ❒ Feeling that you need to keep a clear separation between items that are "clean" and "dirty" (e.g., having "inside clothes" and "outside clothes")
- ❒ Worrying that someone will "contaminate" or "rub off" on you in some way (e.g., taking on undesirable personality traits or characteristics of someone else)
- ❒ Worrying about the risks of certain foods or food preparation (e.g., salmonella, food bacteria, expiration dates)

FEAR OF HARM OR BAD THINGS HAPPENING

- ❒ Fearing that you might harm yourself, someone else, or an animal—either on purpose or by accident
- ❒ Worrying that you will do something bad impulsively or without thinking
- ❒ Worrying that you may have harmed yourself or someone else (and often replaying past events in your mind to check for this)
- ❒ Fearing that you will be responsible for something bad happening (e.g., someone else dies due to your mistake or neglect)
- ❒ Fearing the use of sharp objects (e.g., scissors, knives) because you worry that you could hurt yourself or someone else
- ❒ Seeing scary, violent, or horrific images in your head
- ❒ Fearing the *feeling* of anxiety and its related physical sensations (also called *anxiety sensitivity*) because you believe you can't tolerate it or that something else bad will happen as a result
- ❒ Worrying that you will be stuck with certain OCD thoughts forever (e.g., "What if I'm always thinking about _________?")
- ❒ Fearing that you will go "crazy" or become psychotic

FEAR OF DOING SOMETHING EMBARRASSING OR INAPPROPRIATE

- ❒ Fearing that you will blurt things out inappropriately (e.g., screaming "fire" in a movie theater; cursing out loud in a place of worship)
- ❒ Fearing that you will do something to embarrass yourself publicly (e.g., showing your private parts; taking off clothes in public; getting sick or fainting in front of peers)
- ❒ Fearing that you will exhibit embarrassing physical symptoms (e.g., sweating, shaking)
- ❒ Fearing that you will be "canceled" for doing or saying something inappropriate (e.g., making racist or sexist remarks or insensitive comments)
- ❒ Worrying that you will stare at others in a socially inappropriate way (e.g., staring excessively at someone's private parts; staring at something else unique about someone, like a disability)

RELATIONSHIP FEARS

- ❒ Having doubts about relationships or your feelings in these relationships (e.g., "Do I really love my family members?"; "Am I really happy with my group of friends?"; "Do I want to be with my girlfriend/boyfriend?"; "Are my feelings real or genuine?")
- ❒ Fearing that you are making the "wrong" choice in romantic relationships or friendships (e.g., "Should I be friends with this person?"; "Is this relationship 'right' for me?"; "Could there be someone else out there that's a better fit for me?")
- ❒ Focusing on perceived flaws in others, such as their behavior, appearance, or personality, and worrying that these flaws mean that they are incompatible as relationship partners or friends

INTRUSIVE SEXUAL THOUGHTS

- ❒ Having sexual thoughts or images that bother you (e.g., having thoughts of family members, friends, or teachers that you feel are inappropriate)
- ❒ Having sexual thoughts or images that might be considered weird, bizarre, or taboo (e.g., seeing images of private parts; having thoughts about touching an animal's genitals; having sexual thoughts related to objects)
- ❒ Worrying that you might accidentally touch or grab someone inappropriately (e.g., on their bottom)
- ❒ Worrying that you might harm someone sexually, even though you don't want to
- ❒ Worrying about having unwanted sexual feelings in your body (i.e., having sexual impulses or feeling arousal) and whether that might mean something about you
- ❒ Having preoccupations related to puberty (e.g., concerns that puberty will bring on sexual thoughts or desires that one finds to be confusing, bad, or sinful)
- ❒ Having doubts or concerns about sexuality or gender identity (e.g., "What if I never feel sure about my sexuality?") that are often tied to efforts to check, research, or reassure oneself to alleviate any feelings of doubt

EXCESSIVE SAVING OR DIFFICULTY GETTING RID OF THINGS

- ❒ Having difficulty discarding things due to a fear of making the wrong decision, which may lead to feelings of regret—often because such decisions are irreversible
- ❒ Excessive saving of learning materials (e.g., books, classwork) just in case you need them someday, often tied to an urge to preserve access to knowledge or information that you might want later (e.g., "I need to keep all my past notes, because I might forget something important, and I won't remember unless I can look at them again")
- ❒ Compiling or saving digital resources (e.g., pictures, screenshots, documents, files)
- ❒ Picking up objects that most people would pass by (often due to an inflated sense of responsibility or a desire to prevent harm)

- ❒ Having difficulty getting rid of items that have sentimental value or feeling the need to preserve certain memories (discarding such items may make you feel that you are losing an important part of yourself, and worrying that you'll feel "incomplete" or that something will be "missing" if you get rid of them)
- ❒ Having difficulty discarding items because you believe that the items have feelings, which is referred to as *anthropomorphism* (e.g., "If I get rid of some stuffed animals but not others, the discarded ones will feel unloved and rejected")
- ❒ Having difficulty discarding things because you feel a need to do so in the "right" way (e.g., removing personal or identifying information; insisting that items be properly recycled; ensuring that batteries or needles are properly disposed)
- ❒ Having difficulty getting rid of things even if they're not necessary (e.g., receipts, wrappers, notes with random details or information) because you think you won't be able to cope with not having access to them or want to be able to refer back to or double-check them
- ❒ Purchasing items because you're concerned that the items are one-of-a-kind, that you'll regret not doing so, or that you won't be able to find the item again

EXISTENTIAL AND PHILOSOPHICAL SYMPTOMS

- ❒ Thinking about the meaning of life (e.g., "What is the meaning of life?"; "Why are we here?")
- ❒ Attempting to figure out a sense of purpose (e.g., "What is my purpose in life?"; "What should I be doing with my time on earth?")
- ❒ Thinking about what is "real" in this life and worrying that life is nothing more than a dream (e.g., "Who am I?"; "What if nothing is real?")
- ❒ Thinking about death, dying, and the afterlife (e.g., "What happens after we die?")
- ❒ Thinking about space or the size of the universe (e.g., "We are so small in comparison to the universe"; "Does the universe have a beginning or end?")

"JUST-RIGHT" SYMPTOMS

- ❒ Feeling mentally or physically "off" if things aren't a certain way
- ❒ Repeatedly touching, tapping, or saying things over again, either a certain number of times or until it feels "just right"
- ❒ Organizing or arranging your objects (e.g., toys, books, closet) to the point that it causes significant distress if things are not arranged in a particular way
- ❒ Needing "evenness" or "symmetry" (e.g., feeling that whatever you do with your right hand needs to be done with your left hand; needing your laces on both shoes to be tied with the same degree of tightness)
- ❒ Repeating something in your head or under your breath until you get a feeling that it is "just right"
- ❒ Asking family members or others to repeat things until they sound "just right"

SUPERSTITIOUS SYMPTOMS (MAGICAL THINKING)

- ❒ Only using lucky numbers (and avoiding unlucky numbers)
- ❒ Associating certain colors with being good or bad
- ❒ Avoiding stepping on cracks
- ❒ Avoiding walking under ladders or being near black cats
- ❒ "Knocking on wood" to try to prevent something bad from happening
- ❒ Believing that if you think or say something, it makes it more likely to come true
- ❒ Believing that one behavior is necessary to prevent something unrelated from happening (e.g., "If I don't blink my eyes three times when I have a bad thought about my dad, something bad will happen to him," "If I don't say a certain phrase to undo a bad thought, something bad will happen")

BODY HYPERAWARENESS SYMPTOMS

- ❒ Constantly checking in with your bodily functions (e.g., breathing, swallowing, blinking) to make sure that they're working properly
- ❒ Inspecting your body to make sure nothing is wrong (e.g., physically examining body for signs of illness; checking heart rate)
- ❒ Checking your urge to use the bathroom (e.g., repeatedly attempting to pee at bedtime or before long car rides; excessively squeezing your bowels to see if you need to have a bowel movement)
- ❒ Monitoring your thoughts, feelings, and bodily sensations (e.g., "Am I still thinking about _________?"; "Does my head still hurt?"; "Am I feeling depressed?"; "Do I feel nauseous?")
- ❒ Worrying that you smell or give off a bad body odor

MORALITY OR RELIGION SYMPTOMS

- ❒ Feeling that you always have to do the "right" thing
- ❒ Worrying that you'll lie, say the wrong thing, break a rule, or do something illegal (e.g., that you'll accidentally ingest alcohol or drugs)
- ❒ Confessing potential sins or wrongs due to excessive feelings of guilt
- ❒ Worrying that you'll steal things, either on impulse or by accident
- ❒ Worrying that you didn't say your prayers accurately or had offensive thoughts about God
- ❒ Adhering to religious rules beyond what others in your religious community follow
- ❒ Having fears related to Satan, demons, ghosts, or the paranormal (e.g., fear of being possessed by an evil spirit; fear of being cursed; fear of summoning spirits or being haunted in some way)
- ❒ Fearing going to hell or being eternally damned

PERFECTIONISM SYMPTOMS

- ❒ Worrying about academics (e.g., grades, tests, homework, assignments)
- ❒ Reviewing things to make sure you didn't make a mistake or miss something (e.g., checking homework, rereading emails and text messages, reviewing assignments) 
- ❒ Feeling like you need to perform certain behaviors, skills, or activities perfectly (e.g., gymnastics routine, sports, music, art)
- ❒ Taking notes, making lists, or planning (e.g., weekly schedule, to-do list)
- ❒ Being focused on your appearance, grooming, or clothing

NEEDING TO TELL OR EXPLAIN THINGS ACCURATELY

- ❒ Describing past situations at length when you talk to others so they can give you the most-informed advice or response (e.g., needing to tell parents complete details about something that happened so they can give you reassurance about it)
- ❒ Feeling compelled to confess supposed wrongdoings to others "just in case" you did something wrong
- ❒ Overexplaining what you mean to clarify or justify your actions (e.g., providing unnecessary details to "correct" any potential misunderstanding; repeatedly explaining your reasoning to be sure that someone did not misunderstand you)
- ❒ Saying things as quickly as possible when you talk to others, even if it means interrupting, because you don't want to risk forgetting them
- ❒ Overapologizing due to concerns that you may have done or said something offensive
- ❒ Sharing your plan for something (e.g., how you'll spend your time; how you'll approach a project or your homework) in order to get approval from others about it

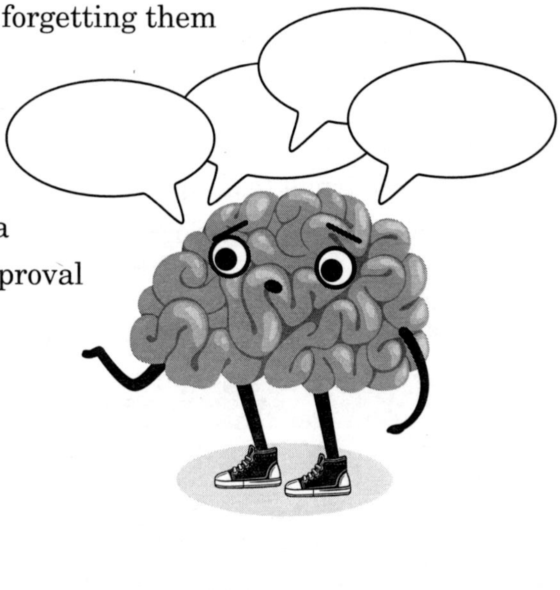

NEEDING TO KNOW OR REMEMBER

- ❒ Making an excessive effort to remember small, often unimportant details or pieces of information so you can recall them later (e.g., license plates, details of a sign or billboard, things others have said)
- ❒ Ruminating about whether you accurately recall or interpreted something that happened in the past (e.g., "Do I remember this correctly?")
- ❒ Taking notes, writing things down, or taking physical pictures of items to be sure you don't miss anything important, or so you can look at them later to check something
- ❒ Worrying that you'll forget something significant (e.g., deadline, personal detail) that could have serious consequences
- ❒ Needing to "review" or "go over" information (e.g., notes, instructions) to ensure accuracy or understanding

NEEDING TO SEEK REASSURANCE

- ❒ Asking loved ones if anything is wrong so they can reassure you that things are fine (e.g., asking others for forgiveness; asking others if they are upset with you)
- ❒ Questioning your teachers or friends (e.g., confirming that you understand something properly in class; seeking reassurance that you completed a task correctly)
- ❒ Seeking confirmation from others in relation to safety (e.g., wanting reassurance that nothing bad will happen; needing to know that the door is locked; asking whether something is contaminated or will make you sick)
- ❒ Asking others for confirmation that you made the "right" choice or the "best" decision
- ❒ Seeking validation that you are a good or moral person (e.g., "Did I do the right thing?"; "Does this thought make me a bad person?")
- ❒ Doing online research to try to reduce your anxiety or figure something out (e.g., trying to determine whether a physical symptom means something is

wrong with your health; searching for information to confirm that you made the "right" decision)

- ❒ Seeking validation about your appearance (e.g., "Do I look okay?"; "Do I look nervous?")
- ❒ Asking about worst-case scenarios and what would happen as a result (e.g., "What if . . .")

CHECKING RITUALS

- ❒ Checking things around the house to make sure that nothing bad will happen (e.g., checking that the hair dryer is unplugged to avoid a fire; checking locks and doors to avoid someone breaking in)
- ❒ Checking too much to make sure you didn't miss anything important (e.g., a homework assignment; a friend's birthday)
- ❒ Checking to make sure you don't (or didn't) lose anything
- ❒ Checking to make sure that something bad didn't happen to other people (e.g., "Did I hurt you?")

ROUTINES AND REPEATING RITUALS

- ❒ Doing things repetitively (e.g., walking in and out of doors; turning light switches on and off; going up and down stairs; opening and closing cabinets)
- ❒ Rereading things (e.g., doubting whether you understood a paragraph fully; feeling concerned that you missed something in a chapter)
- ❒ Rewriting or fixing your handwriting (e.g., making words neater or letters look "perfect")
- ❒ Doing your daily activities in a ritualized way (e.g., getting dressed in a certain order; having a specific and inflexible bedtime routine)

THINKING RITUALS (MENTAL COMPULSIONS)

- ❒ Thinking something through in order to justify something, solve something, make a decision, or reach a conclusion or answer
- ❒ Reviewing past conversations in your head to try to remember what was said or how others responded
- ❒ Obsessing about a "real event" from the past to determine whether it means something (e.g., "Does this say something about me?") or if you handled it right
- ❒ Getting an image in your mind about something that didn't happen and then obsessing about whether it *actually* did happen and you just forgot about it
- ❒ Replaying past events in your mind to be sure of what happened (e.g., whether you did something wrong, offended someone, or did something harmful)
- ❒ Taking "mental images" to help you remember things (e.g., taking a mental picture of a door lock so you can think back to the picture later to confirm that you locked it; staring at the dial on the stove in order to get a mental image in your mind that it's off)
- ❒ Playing out future events or hypothetical situations in your mind to think about how to handle them (e.g., social situations, crisis scenarios)
- ❒ Mentally reviewing your to-do list so you don't forget things
- ❒ Attempting to push thoughts out of your head, cancel them out, or neutralize them (e.g., trying to counteract a "bad" or scary thought by replacing it with an opposite "good" or happy thought)
- ❒ "Testing" how things make you feel or whether you like or dislike something (e.g., trying to figure out if you feel disgusted or excited when you have an inappropriate thought; purposely watching a kissing scene in a movie to confirm that you think kissing is "gross")

COUNTING RITUALS

- ❒ Counting your steps while walking, sometimes in effort to end on a certain number
- ❒ Counting objects in the room, or to ensure that nothing is missing

- ❒ Counting in specific multiples or patterns (e.g., by twos or fives) in a way that "feels right"
- ❒ Counting during certain routines or activities (e.g., while brushing teeth) to feel sure that the task was completed thoroughly

AVOIDANCE

- ❒ Avoiding situations or places that might trigger intrusive thoughts or worries (e.g., a specific restaurant, a certain road, a place of worship)
- ❒ Avoiding specific movies, TV shows, books, or articles because they trigger obsessions or anxiety
- ❒ Avoiding situations that make you feel the need to do rituals (e.g., not doing homework because you constantly reread and rewrite your answers; not leaving the house because it might trigger the urge to do checking rituals)
- ❒ Avoiding certain foods or drinks due to concerns that they'll harm you in some way (e.g., fearing contamination or illness; worrying about the impact that caffeine, sugar, or other substances may have on your body; worrying that certain foods might cause allergic reactions or skin breakouts)
- ❒ Avoiding certain people that might trigger intrusive thoughts (e.g., staying away from someone you think is contaminated; avoiding someone who triggers intrusive sexual thoughts)
- ❒ Avoiding activities that could lead to mistakes or bad outcomes (e.g., avoiding starting projects; avoiding making decisions)
- ❒ Avoiding daily activities, neglecting hygiene, or procrastinating to try to "escape" or get away from obsessive thoughts (e.g., excessive sleeping to avoid dealing with bothersome thoughts; scrolling through your phone to distract yourself from intrusive thoughts; not showering because your washing compulsions are so tedious to complete)

RITUALS INVOLVING FAMILY MEMBERS

- ❑ Having family members participate in your OCD rituals (e.g., checking things for you; wiping your bottom for you after you go to the bathroom)
- ❑ Asking family members to do things for you that you otherwise could do yourself, because it allows you to avoid dealing with your OCD (e.g., getting certain items for you because it's a lot of effort for you to get them yourself)
- ❑ Having family members change the family routine so your OCD isn't triggered (e.g., changing the time that you do certain things; taking a different driving route)

Are there any other bothersome thoughts, images, or repetitive behaviors that weren't listed above? If so, write them here.

1. ________________________________

2. ________________________________

3. ________________________________

4. ________________________________

5. ________________________________

As you can see, there are a lot of different ways that a *tricky, sticky, picky* brain can affect you. However, these are just some of the most common symptoms that come up, and you may have other worries and concerns that are not even included on this list. That's because OCD symptoms can be related to anything. What's more is that a lot of kids experience a mashup of different themes of OCD symptoms. For example, they may feel like they have to wash their hands over and over again until it "feels right," or they may feel like they have to say things a certain way to prevent something bad from happening. Either way, if you have noticed some of these concerns in your own experience, the next step is to make a plan to do something about it! In the next chapter, we'll begin discussing strategies that can help you take control of OCD so that it stops bothering you so much.

CHAPTER 3

Understanding the Thought-Feeling-Behavior Cycle

As you know, it can be super frustrating to have to deal with a *tricky, sticky, picky* brain. The good news is that there are amazing strategies to get your brain to stop picking on you so much! Now, you may be thinking, "Well, they won't work for me. I'm different." I had that thought once too, and I was skeptical that anything could help. However, thousands of kids have used these strategies and found them to work. That means if you give these strategies your all, there's a very good chance that you can get your *tricky, sticky, picky* brain to stop bothering you so much. Let's start by going over the relationship between thoughts, feelings, and behaviors, which will help you understand some of the strategies we'll be talking about.

The Relationship Between Thoughts, Feelings, and Behaviors

Did you know that our thoughts, feelings, and behaviors are all related to each other? For example, the way we *think* contributes to how we *feel*, and the way we feel often influences our *behavior*. Scientists use the fancy term *cognitive behavioral model* to describe this cycle of how thoughts, feelings, and behaviors are all related.

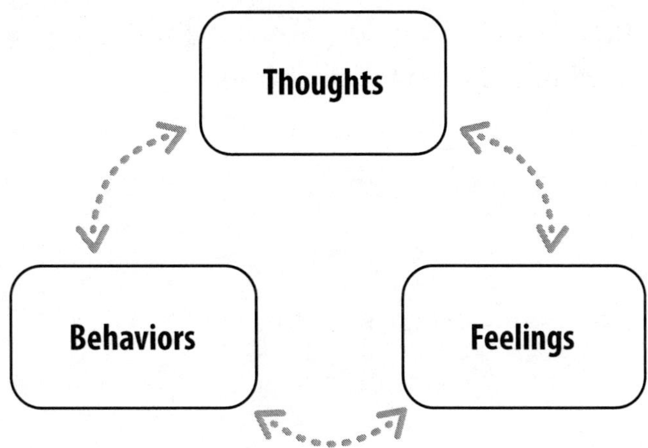

Here's an example to explain this relationship. Let's imagine that you're at school, and your teacher tells you that your class has won the school fundraiser, so you'll be having an ice cream sundae party in about an hour, just after lunch. You think to yourself, "I can't wait to eat ice cream! It's my favorite dessert!" In turn, you feel happy and excited, so you start squirming in your seat, you have difficulty focusing, and your mouth starts watering just thinking about the ice cream you're about to eat. If we break down what happened, you can see that your thought led to your feelings, which led to your behaviors.

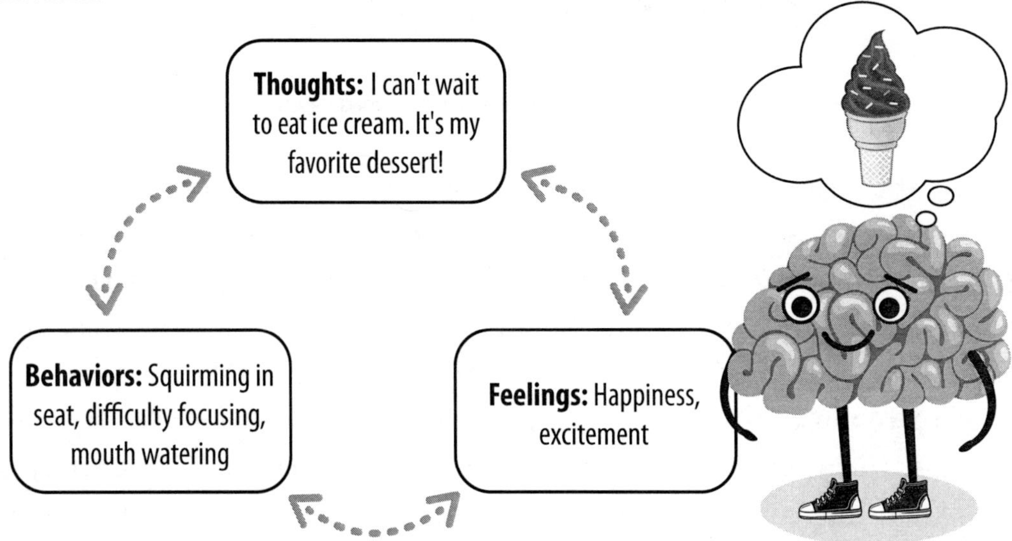

Now, what if you were lactose intolerant and couldn't eat ice cream? You might then find that your thoughts, feelings, and behaviors would be a lot different. See, not everyone experiences the same cycles of thoughts, feelings, and behaviors—meaning that the same situation can lead to different thoughts, feelings, and behaviors for different people. Let's discuss how this could happen, using dogs as an example.

I personally love dogs. They are usually fun, energetic, and pretty cuddly. If I see a dog playfully catching a ball at the park, I might think to myself, "It is so cute. I want to play with it!" This might elicit a feeling of excitement, which may lead me to eagerly walk up to the owner and ask to pet the dog. My thought upon seeing the dog impacted how I felt as well as what I did in terms of my behavior.

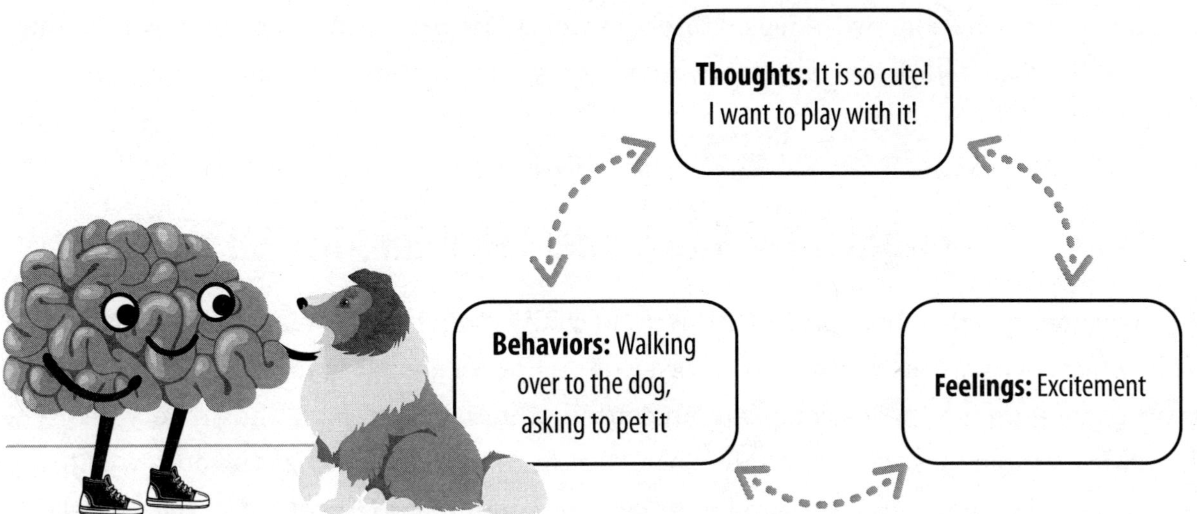

On the other hand, let's think about what might happen if someone is afraid of dogs. Things will go differently when they see a dog at the park, even if it is a cute and fluffy five-pound dog. First, they might have a variety of unhelpful and scary thoughts, like "I'm in danger" or "It's going to bite me." In turn, they'll feel afraid and anxious, which will lead them to try to escape the situation by leaving the park.

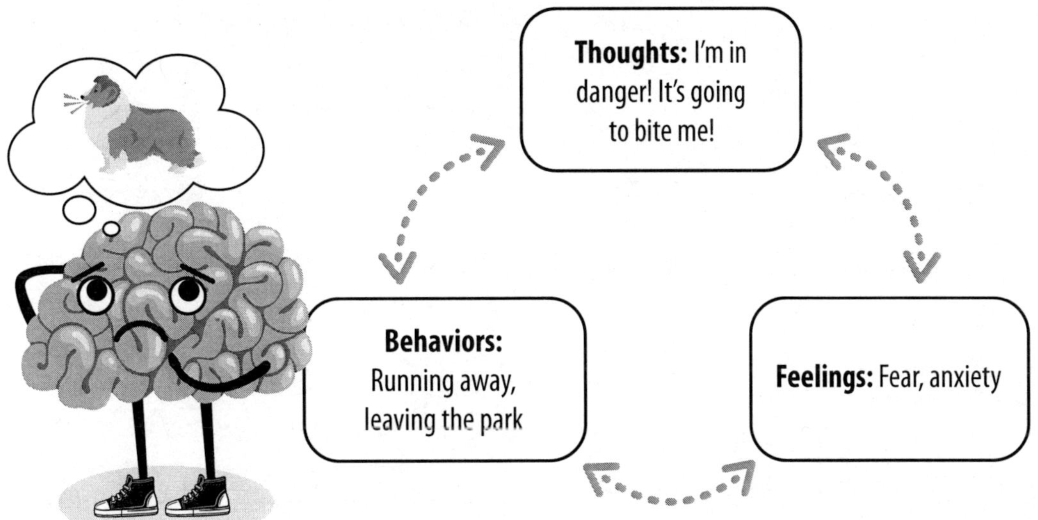

Once this person leaves the park, they'll think to themselves, "Whew! I'm glad I got out of there! Something really bad could have happened with that dog." As a result, the next time they're around a dog, they'll likely end up doing the same thing, which is to avoid the dog again, as that's the only way they know to handle a situation like this to feel less scared. This is often the cycle of what happens when someone is afraid of something: They do what is familiar to them in order to feel better as soon as possible, which in this situation, is to avoid the dog. As a result, their thoughts ("I'm in danger"), feelings (fear), and behaviors (running away) stay the same since they don't give themself the chance to see if things could go differently. If this cycle continues, they'll keep avoiding situations with dogs. Unfortunately, this prevents them from overcoming their fear of dogs and potentially learning that they can handle, or even enjoy, being around dogs.

Thoughts, Feelings, and Behaviors in OCD

Let's now get specific about what this cycle looks like when you have OCD. With OCD, whenever you encounter a specific situation or trigger, it leads you to have certain thoughts (i.e., obsessions), which cause bothersome feelings like anxiety, fear, discomfort, embarrassment, or shame. Your brain then tells you that the only way to feel better is to engage in a certain behavior (i.e., compulsion) to get rid of the anxiety or distress. Since you are eager to feel better and move on, you often do the compulsion that your brain tells you to do.

Here's an example of how this might look for a child who is anxious about a robber breaking into their home, so they repeatedly check that the front door is locked.

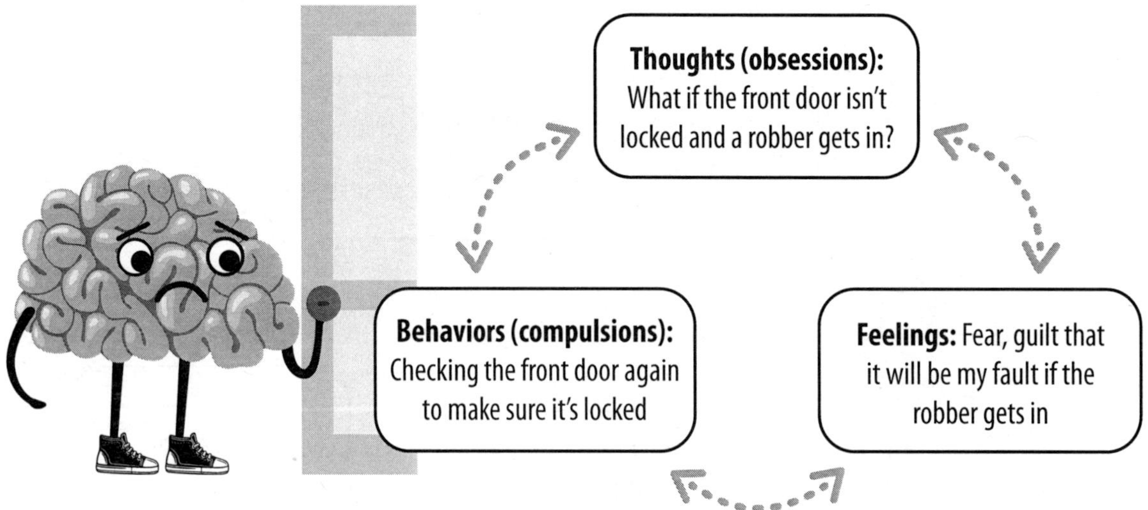

In this example, you can see that the child engages in the compulsion of physically checking the door lock. Physical compulsions like this are often fairly easy to identify. However, with OCD, sometimes the behavior in the thought-feeling-behavior cycle comes in the form of a *mental compulsion*, which is a behavior that occurs in your mind. Mental compulsions can involve replaying past conversations to feel sure of what was said, reviewing past situations to reassure yourself that you handled something the "right" way, trying to replace "bad" thoughts with "good" thoughts, or repeating certain words or phrases in your head until it feels right. Many kids with OCD aren't even aware when they engage in these mental behaviors since they aren't visible. You may even feel as if they happen automatically! They're still behaviors though, and if you can recognize them, you can eventually learn to challenge them.

Here's an example of what the thought-feeling-behavior cycle might look like for a child who has the mental compulsion of replacing "bad" thoughts with "good" thoughts.

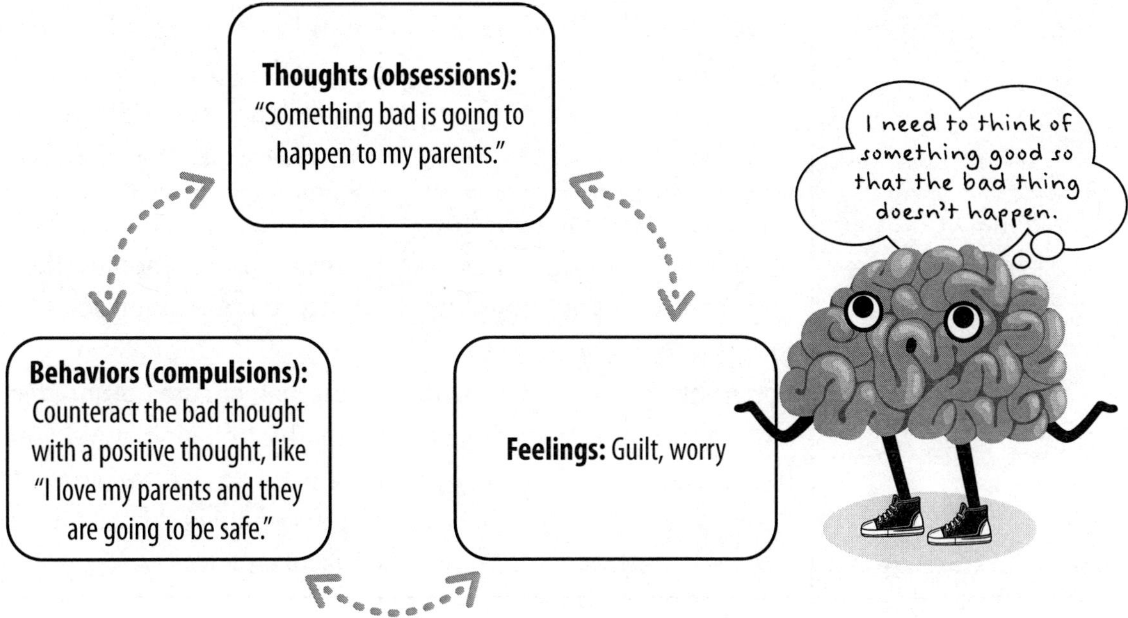

And here's an example of what the cycle might look like for a kid who has the mental compulsion of trying to figure out whether or not they said something inappropriate in a past conversation.

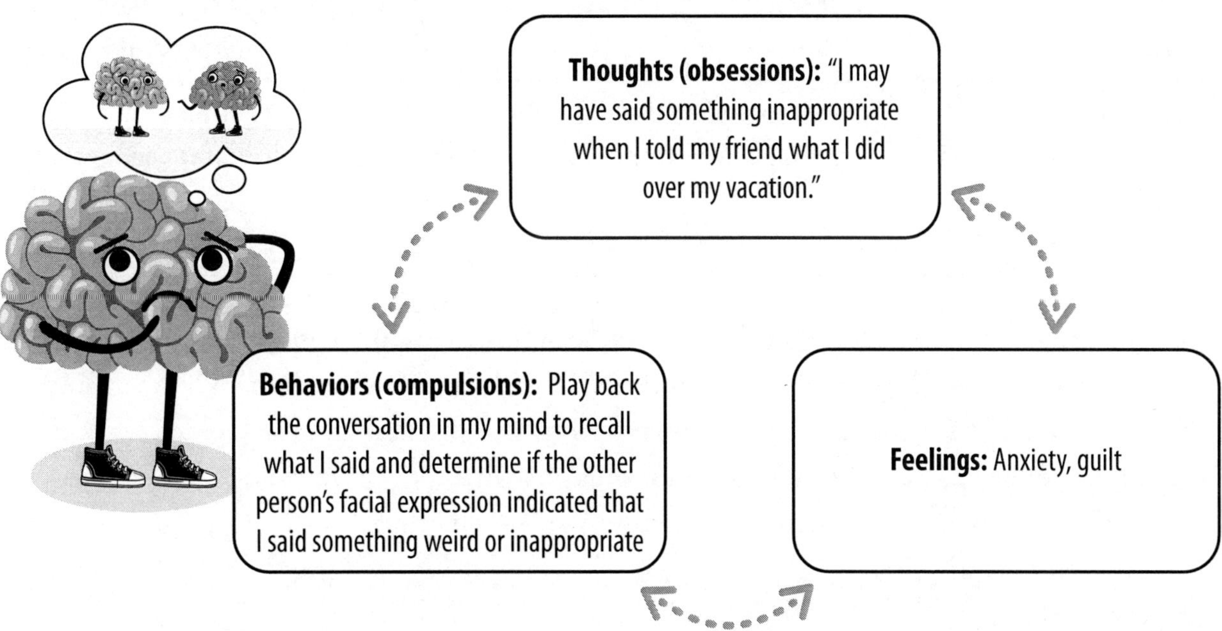

Remember from the previous chapter that any obsession can be linked with any compulsion and vice versa. That means that the same obsession can be linked with physical or mental compulsions, as shown with several examples in the following table.

Obsession	Physical Compulsion	Mental Compulsion
Worry that you may have hurt someone's feelings	Ask the person for reassurance so you feel sure that you did not offend them	Replay the interaction in your mind to try to recall if you said something offensive or if their body language indicated that you said something offensive
Concern that you could have a serious disease	Physically examine your body for signs of a serious illness (e.g., checking your body for lumps due to concerns that you might have cancer, using a heart monitor to check your heart rate)	Hyperfocus on your bodily sensations and monitor them to try to figure out if something feels "off" (e.g., analyzing whether you are getting deep breaths; "thinking about your thinking" to determine whether your cognitive skills are intact or worsening)
Need to figure out the meaning of life	Research online about the meaning of life	Ruminate about the meaning of life to try to find an answer
Concern that you're a bad person because you had a thought that you deemed immoral	Say extra prayers aloud to neutralize or cancel out the thought that you found inappropriate	Mentally review all of the reasons you are a "good person" to reassure yourself that you are not immoral
Worry that you'll be responsible for a fire if you forgot to unplug your hair dryer	Check to make sure the hair dryer is off and unplugged	Try to recall the image of yourself unplugging the hair dryer

Now that you understand the relationship between thoughts, feelings, and behaviors, you can see how these unhelpful cycles will just go on and on. When similar triggers or situations come up, you remember what you did last time to feel better (e.g., checking the door lock, counteracting a bad thought with a positive thought), and you end up doing the same thing again and again. As a result, your *tricky, sticky, picky* brain gets even stronger (i.e., more *tricky, sticky, and picky*) over time, unless you do something to change it.

Subjective Units of Distress Scale

To understand how OCD gets stronger over time, it's helpful to use a *subjective units of distress (SUD) scale*. A SUD scale is basically just a visual tool that allows you to rate how much anxiety or discomfort you are feeling inside. It's a way to rate the strength or intensity of your feelings. Some thoughts elicit a little bit of distress, whereas others elicit a lot of distress. On a SUD scale, you usually rate your distress on a scale from 0 to 10, where 0 is "no distress at all" and 10 is "the most distress you could possibly experience."

10	Debilitating anxiety or distress
9	Extreme anxiety or distress
8	Very severe anxiety or distress
7	Severe anxiety or distress
6	Moderate to severe anxiety or distress
5	Moderate anxiety or distress
4	Mild to moderate anxiety or distress
3	Mild anxiety or distress
2	Minimal anxiety or distress
1	Very slight anxiety or distress
0	No anxiety or distress

Now, let's explain how to use a SUD scale using the previous example of a child who is anxious about a robber breaking into their home. Whenever this child obsesses about whether the front door is locked (thought), it causes their anxiety (feeling) to increase (SUD = 8). In response, they compulsively check the front door (behavior) to make sure no one is able to get in. This lowers their anxiety a good bit (SUD = 2) for the time being. However, the next night, the child again worries that a robber could get in if the front door isn't locked, so their anxiety goes up (SUD = 8). They remember that they felt less anxious after they checked the door lock last night, so they decide to do that again to feel better. This lowers their anxiety once more (SUD = 3), and they go off to sleep.

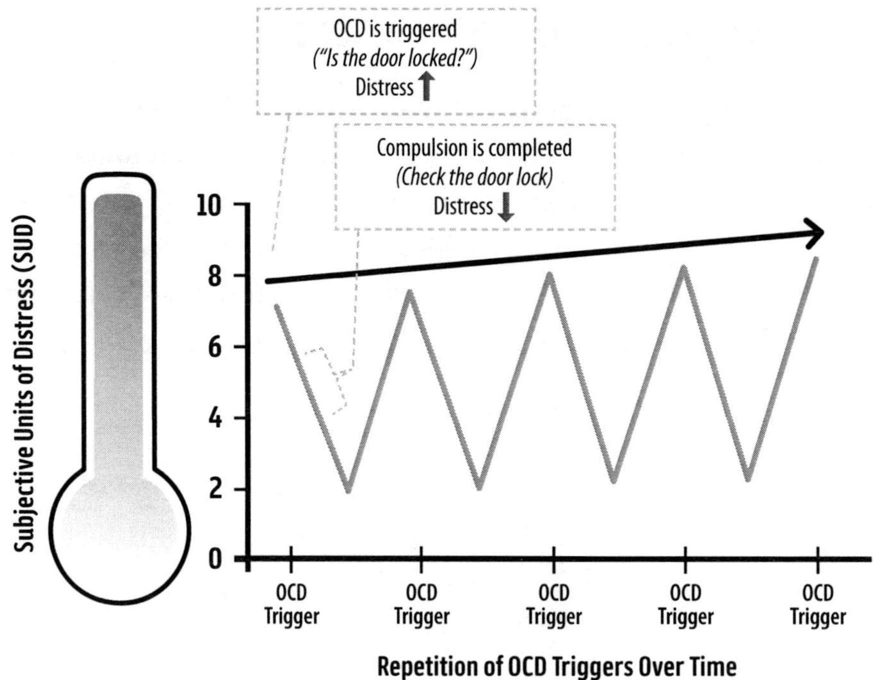

This OCD cycle tends to continue and usually worsens over time. That's because you come to believe that the only way to feel less anxious and to possibly prevent something bad from happening—like a robber getting in—is to do the compulsion. Further, since OCD is *tricky*, it tricks you into doing even more compulsive behaviors in order to feel satisfied. Perhaps it starts by telling you to check the door once, but then suddenly asks you to check it twice or maybe even three or four times. Each time you give in, OCD thinks, "I got them to do what I want . . . let's see what else I can get them to do." It might then tell you that you should have a parent check the door too, just in case you checked it wrong, and so the responsibility doesn't fall just on you. OCD might get even more *picky* with what it asks you to do. For example, it might want you to stare at the door lock and take a "mental picture" so you can think back to that picture later and confirm that you locked it. It might also start telling you that you need to check other things too, like windows, just in case a robber could get in some other way.

Exploring the Relationship Between Obsessions and Compulsions

When considering the child who is anxious about a robber breaking into their home, there seems to be a logical connection between the child's worry (that a robber might get in through an unlocked door) and the compulsion (checking to make sure the door is locked). However, this isn't always the case with OCD. As you've learned, sometimes the rituals don't seem connected at all to whatever you are worried about. In fact, it's incredibly common for the thoughts in OCD to seem confusing, strange, or even inappropriate. And the compulsions and rituals don't always make much sense either! Still, your *tricky, sticky, picky* brain makes them *feel* related, so you feel like you have to do them anyway.

IMPORTANT POINT

Many people with OCD are aware that their thoughts and behaviors are irrational and don't make much sense, but they still have a difficult time challenging them. They still feel compelled to do what OCD wants. If that has been your experience, just know that it is super common and doesn't mean that you'll be any less capable of gaining control over OCD.

For instance, a child with a *tricky, sticky, picky* brain might think that if they hear about something bad (e.g., a car accident on the news), that same bad thing will happen to their own family (obsession) unless they tap on something eight times (compulsion). Since the obsession is quite scary and anxiety-provoking, they'll often do what their *tricky, sticky, picky* brain tells them to do (e.g., tap eight times) in order to feel better. Maybe the child isn't sure if the tapping ritual is really necessary, but they'll do it anyway "just in case." OCD is *tricky* that way, in that it has ways of convincing people to do such things. We'll talk about this more later on.

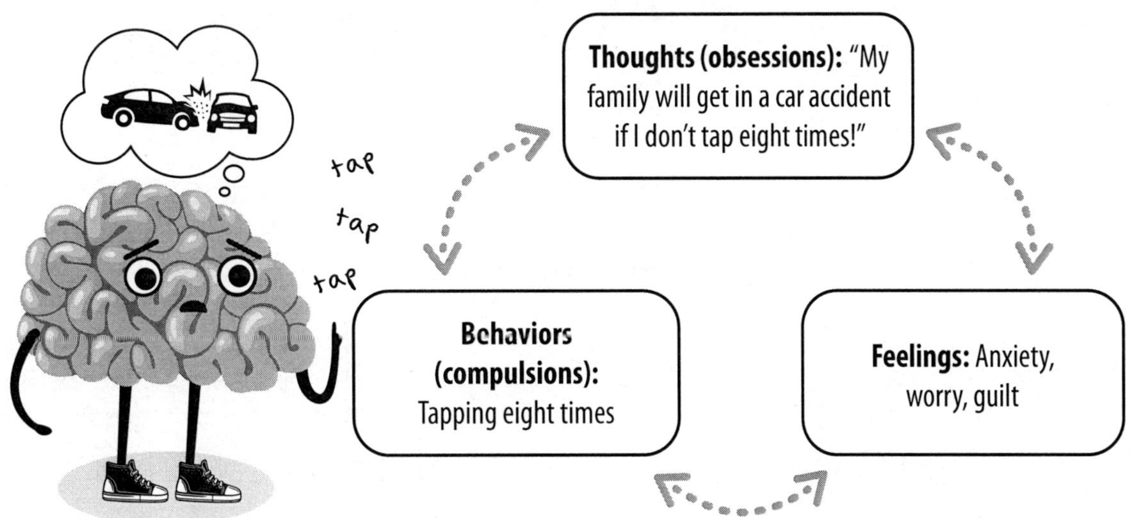

If the child taps eight times and nothing bad happens, they'll probably assume that the tapping ritual kept their family safe. (Or even if they're not sure if the tapping actually made a difference, they aren't willing to risk not doing it.) If similar worries come up in the future, the child will be quick to do their tapping compulsion again since it helped them feel better last time. Remember that this cycle tends to continue and worsen over time, as the child thinks that the only way to feel less anxious, and to possibly prevent harm to their family, is to do their tapping ritual.

Understanding Your OCD Cycle

Hopefully, these examples have helped you understand the OCD cycle. Now it's time to think about how this all applies to *your* OCD. What are some of the cycles that OCD causes you to be stuck in? Write a few of these in the examples here.

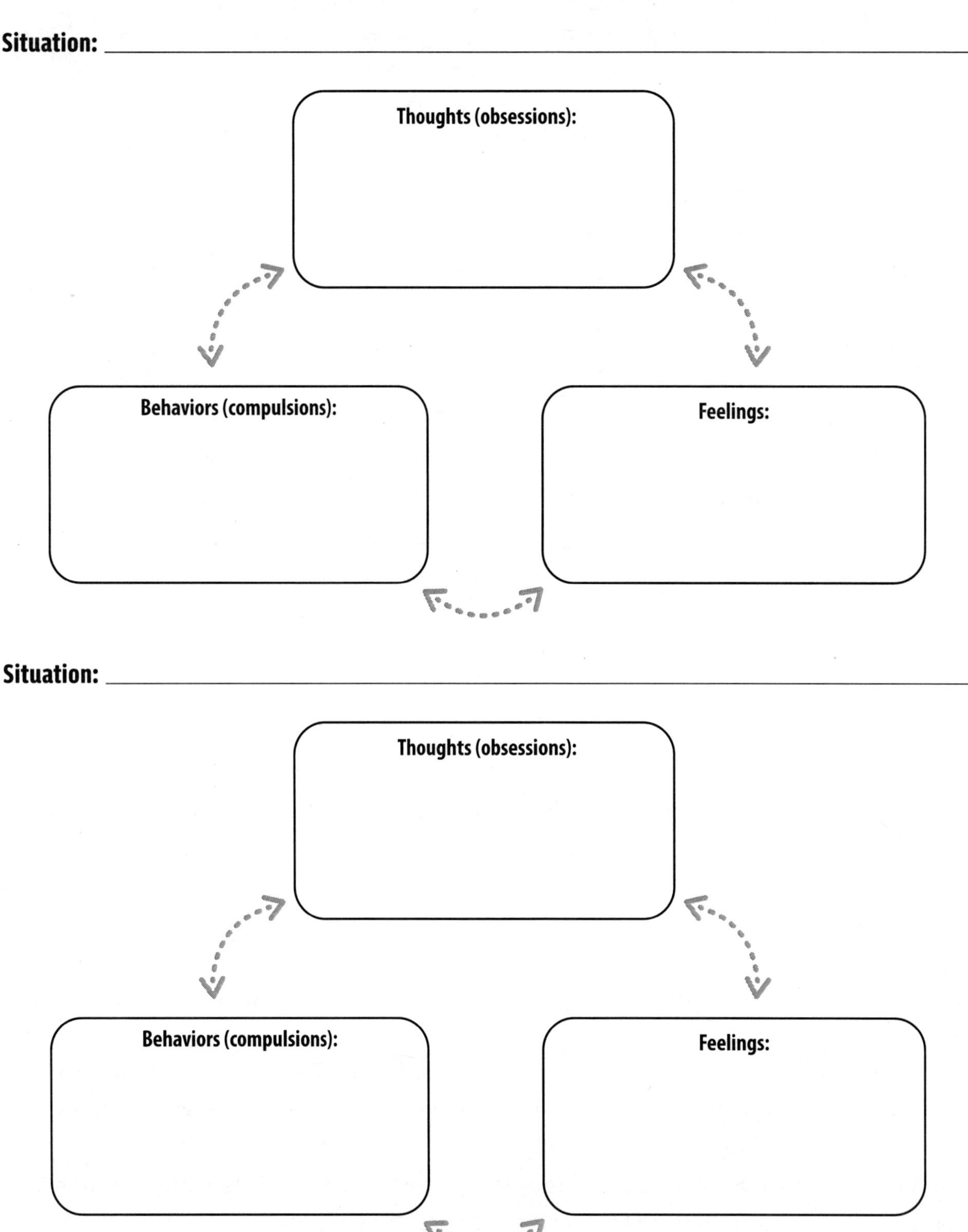

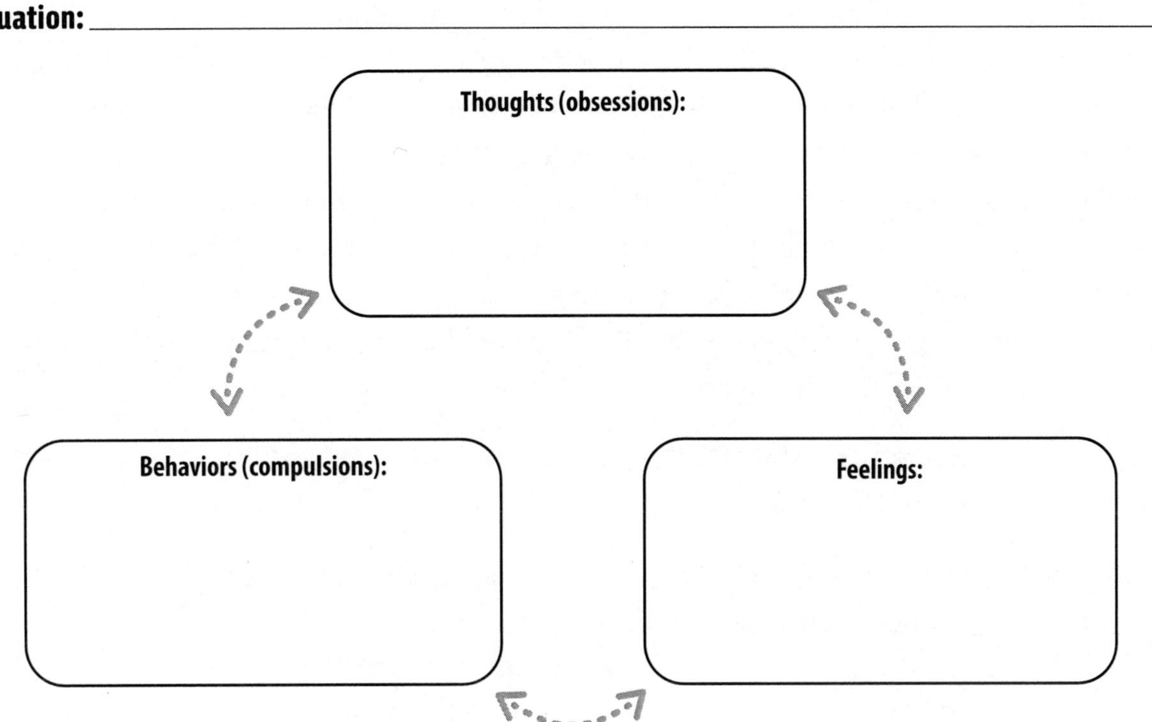

So, if you want to change the thought-feeling-behavior cycle—and if all parts of the cycle are related to each other—where should you start? With thoughts? Feelings? Behaviors? Some people want to *feel* better quickly, so they start by trying to change their feelings. Unfortunately, that doesn't work very well. Just think about it: Have you ever had a time when you were super worried about something and someone else told you, "Don't worry!" Not so helpful, right? If it were just that easy to "not worry," we obviously wouldn't worry! It's just not that easy to simply turn off our feelings.

So, although someone may have good intentions when they tell you not to worry—and there may be *some* things you can do to decrease the intensity of your feelings—it isn't very effective as the main strategy to break an unhelpful thought-feeling-behavior cycle.

Instead of focusing on trying to change your feelings, it is much more effective to identify unhelpful *thoughts* and *behaviors*, and then work to change those where you can.

Let's revisit the person who has a fear of dogs to see how they might start to make changes. Imagine that this person is fed up with their fear of dogs. Perhaps their best friend has some really awesome activities to do at their house, like a pool or an outdoor trampoline, but they've never gone there because their best friend also has a dog. Is there anything they can do to stop letting fear run the show? Absolutely! Let's look at their thought-feeling-behavior cycle again to see where we can intervene. We want to focus on identifying thoughts and behaviors that might *seem* helpful but are actually making things worse. Specifically, we want to consider:

1. Are the thoughts helpful? Do they make good sense? Or are they unhelpful and don't make much sense?
2. Are the behaviors helpful? Do they make good sense? Or are they unhelpful and don't make much sense?

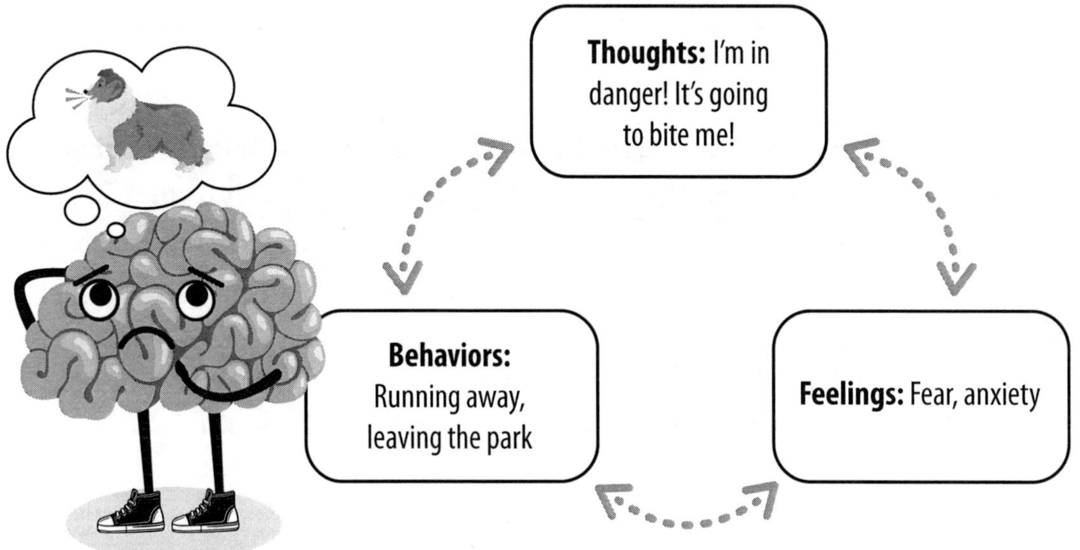

In this example, let's consider the thought "I'm in danger! It's going to bite me!" This thought would cause the person to feel pretty scared. However, if they were to look at the situation more closely, they might be able to recognize that it is very unlikely that this particular dog will cause serious harm. For example, this dog is only five pounds and seems friendly since it's playfully wagging its tail. In fact, it's not doing anything whatsoever to suggest that it is going to bite the person or become aggressive. It's not growling or barking. It's not snarling at the person with sharp teeth. It's not even jumping on them. Therefore, the thought "I'm in danger!" is not helpful, and it doesn't make sense when considering the actual facts of the situation. After checking the facts, it's likely that the person will feel less scared.

Let's also consider the behaviors (running away, leaving the park) to see if these are helpful and make sense in this particular situation. If a five-pound dog were to lunge at someone, is it likely to cause serious harm? Is the dog doing anything to suggest that the person is in immediate danger? If there are other people at the park, do they seem scared of the dog? Would this person miss out on enjoying the park if they left? After considering these questions, this person will hopefully realize that the behavior of running away doesn't make good sense given this particular situation and dog.

After determining that their previous thoughts and behaviors don't make much sense, this person may decide to stay at the park the next time they see this dog, rather than staying away. If they eventually let the dog come closer, they might see that it is a friendly dog who only wants to sniff them. Maybe they will even get the courage to pet the dog, and the dog will wag its tail in return. By recognizing their unhelpful thoughts and doing something different (i.e., changing their behavior), they were able to take steps to break the cycle and work to overcome their fear of dogs. In fact, they learned that what they *expected* would happen (the dog would bite them) was very different from what *actually* happened (the dog was playful and friendly). With this new knowledge, they can finally go over to their best friend's house and enjoy themselves there without letting their fear get in the way.

In the next few chapters, we'll go over these strategies in much more detail so you can start to recognize unhelpful patterns of thinking that serve as clues that your *tricky, sticky, picky* brain is trying to run the show. You'll also learn how changing your behavior can serve as an incredibly powerful method to break the OCD cycle.

CHAPTER 4

Identifying *Tricky* Thinking Traps

Everyone has unhelpful ways of thinking sometimes. But those of us with *tricky, sticky, picky* brains tend to struggle with this more often. It's not something we do on purpose—it's just the way our brains work! The goal of this chapter is to help you figure out when your brain is *tricking* you into believing things that aren't likely or true. We call these *thinking traps*, and they happen when your OCD causes you to automatically think about things in negative or unhelpful ways. Unfortunately, these thinking traps can trick you into feeling even more anxious or upset. *But* . . . if you become aware of these traps, you can then work to change this way of thinking!

"Wait a minute . . . change my thinking? How could I possibly do that? That sounds really tough."

—LUCAS, AGE 10

Changing your thinking may *sound* tough, but it's actually not so difficult after all. It's also a pretty awesome tool to push back on your fears and feel less anxious. The first thing you need to do is identify what types of thinking traps you tend to fall into. You'll find a list of common traps on the next few pages, along with examples to help explain them. Go through this list and check off any traps that you've noticed in your own thinking. Some of these traps are pretty similar to each other, so it's likely you'll check off multiple items. For the items that you've checked off, write an example of how that trap has shown up in your OCD.

Thinking Traps That May Show Up When You Have a *Tricky, Sticky, Picky* Brain

❐ **Catastrophizing:** You think that the worst-case scenario is going to happen and expect disaster! This is sometimes called *what-if thinking*.

Examples:

- "I'm worried about my test tomorrow. I'm going to forget everything I studied."
- You assume your headache is probably due to a brain tumor.
- Your own example: ____

____

____

❐ **Negative glasses:** You only see the negative and overlook the positive in a situation. It's as if the positives don't count. Even when you have a good time (or do well on something), you still focus on the things that went wrong.

Examples:

- You focus on the one question you couldn't answer on the test rather than all of the answers that you did know.
- You have a good time eating out at a restaurant, but you tell yourself that the entire experience was disappointing because they no longer have your favorite item on the menu.
- Your own example: ____

____

____

❒ **Overestimating threat:** You exaggerate the chance that something bad will happen.

Examples:

- "I'll probably get sick if I drink from that glass with a speck on it."
- You worry that you forgot to lock the front door and tell yourself that you're going to get robbed.
- Your own example: ____

____

____

❒ **Intolerance of uncertainty:** You believe that you need to be sure about something in order to be okay. You assume that you can't handle not knowing.

Examples:

- "I can't deal with it if there's a chance that I left the stove on. I need to be sure."
- You aren't able to fall asleep until you know for sure that you submitted your assignment for school.
- Your own example: ____

____

____

❒ **Repetitive thinking:** You think that if something happened one way, it's always going to happen that way.

Examples:

- "I once got sick after eating chicken, so I bet I'll get sick if I eat chicken again."
- You stumbled through a presentation last week, so you assume you're going to mess up next time too.
- Your own example: ____

____

____

❒ **Jumping to conclusions:** You make assumptions about something without all the facts.

Examples:

- "She didn't respond to my text, so she must be mad at me."
- When your teacher asks to talk to you after class, you assume that it must be because you are in trouble rather than other possible reasons (e.g., to praise your participation in class or your recent assignment).
- Your own example: ____

____

____

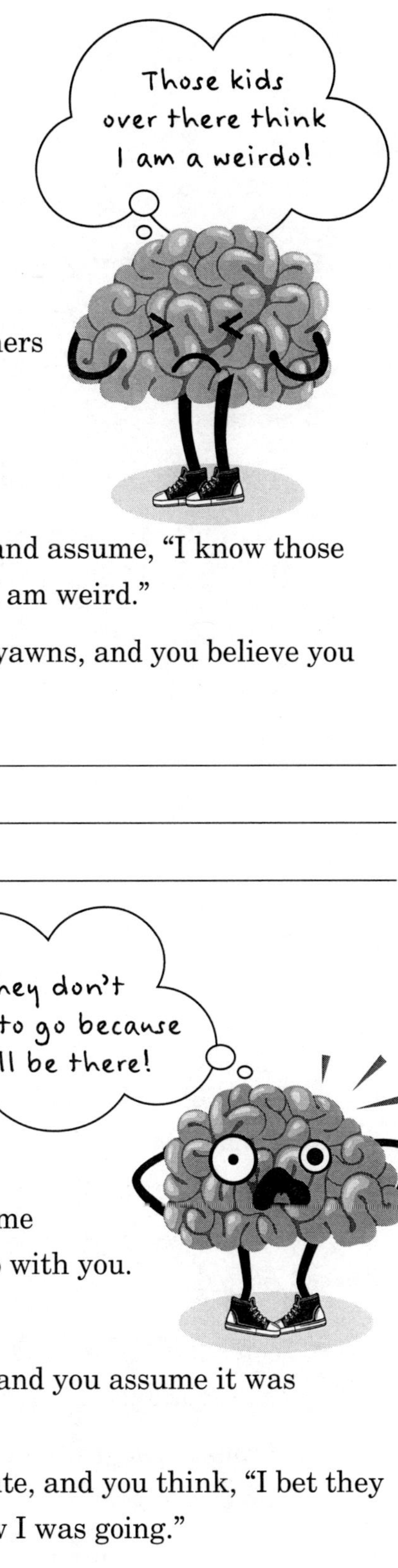

❒ **Mind-reading:** You assume that you know what others are thinking (and often assume that what they're thinking is negative).

Examples:

- You see a group of kids whispering to each other and assume, "I know those kids are talking about me right now. They think I am weird."
- While you are giving a presentation, a classmate yawns, and you believe you are boring him.
- Your own example: ____

❒ **Personalization:** You take things personally or blame yourself for things that may not have anything to do with you.

Examples:

- Your teacher sends out a stern email to the class and you assume it was probably directed at you.
- One of your friends cancels plans at the last minute, and you think, "I bet they didn't want to go to the movies because they knew I was going."
- Your own example: ____

- ❒ **Fortune-telling:** You expect that things will turn out badly, no matter what. It's as if you have a crystal ball that can predict the future.

  Examples:

  - "No one is going to talk to me at the party."
  - You know you get nervous when you perform in front of people, so you expect that you will freeze on stage during your music recital.
  - Your own example: ______________________________

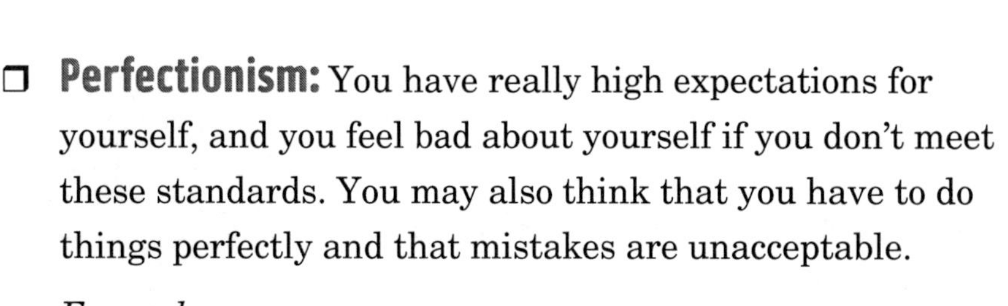

- ❒ **Perfectionism:** You have really high expectations for yourself, and you feel bad about yourself if you don't meet these standards. You may also think that you have to do things perfectly and that mistakes are unacceptable.

  Examples:

  - You believe that getting anything less than 100 percent on a test is unacceptable.
  - "I must always do the right thing to be a good person. Otherwise, I'm not good enough."
  - Your own example: ______________________________

❐ **Should statements:** You impose strict rules about how you and others "should" think or act. These rules are characterized by words like *should*, *must*, *ought*, or *have to*.

Examples:

- You believe you must avoid making any mistakes.
- "I should never have these kinds of thoughts."
- Your own example: ____________________

❐ **All-or-nothing thinking:** You see things as all good or all bad, with no in-between.

Examples:

- If your performance falls short of perfect, you see yourself as a total failure.
- A friend tells you that you are being annoying, so you think, "No one likes me."
- Your own example: ____________________

- [ ] **Inflated responsibility:** You believe that it is your duty to prevent bad things from happening.

  Examples:

  - "If something bad happens to my family, it must be because I missed something with my nighttime rituals."
  - You think you must pick up all of the litter you see or else you are contributing to the demise of the planet.
  - Your own example: ______________________________

    ____

    ____

- [ ] **Overimportance of thoughts:** You believe that all thoughts must mean something, so you should pay attention to them.

  Examples:

  - You had a thought about hurting your sister, so it must mean that you really want to do it.
  - "The fact that I'm having doubts about the trip must mean something. Maybe I shouldn't go."
  - Your own example: ______________________________

    ____

    ____

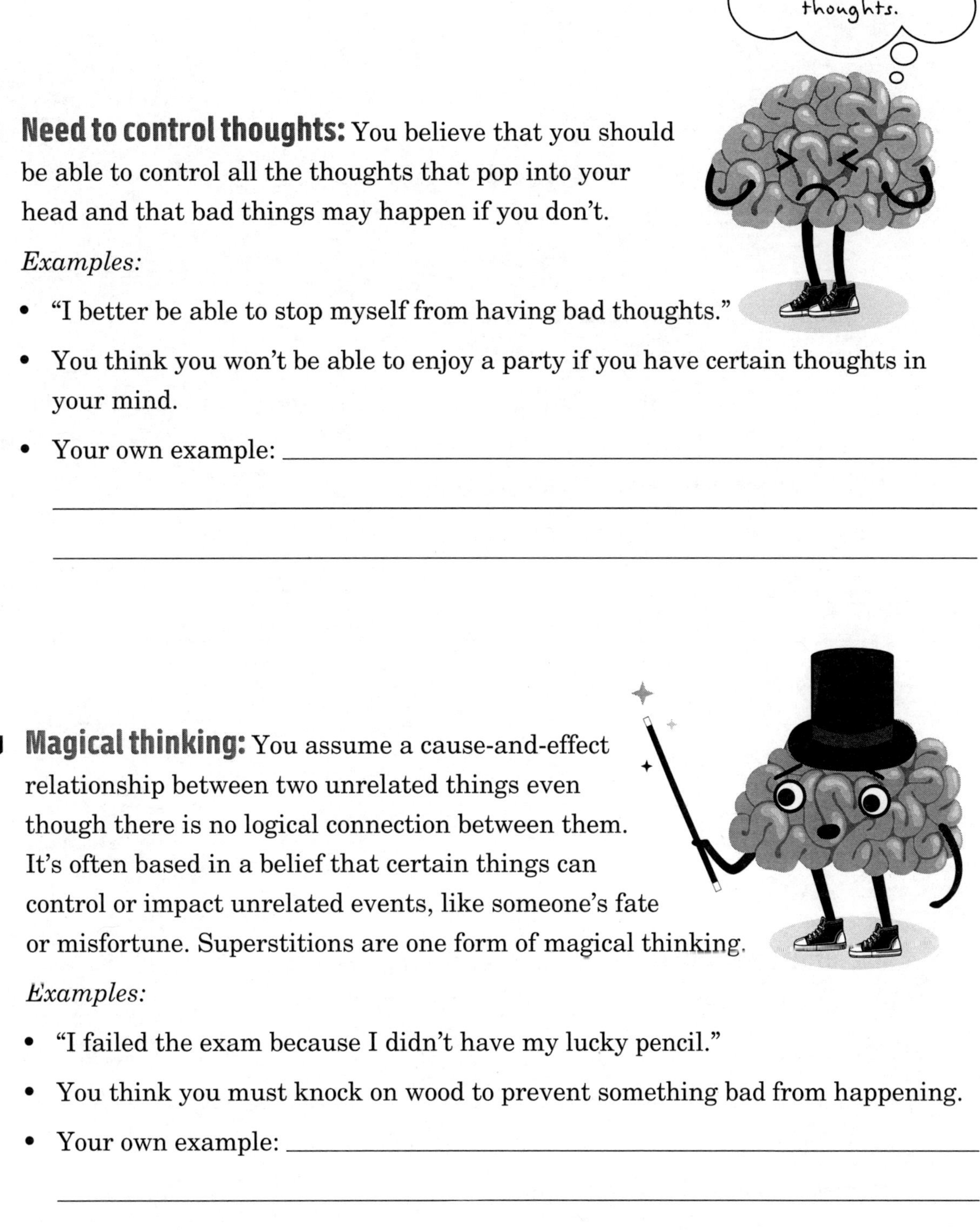

❒ **Need to control thoughts:** You believe that you should be able to control all the thoughts that pop into your head and that bad things may happen if you don't.

Examples:

- "I better be able to stop myself from having bad thoughts."
- You think you won't be able to enjoy a party if you have certain thoughts in your mind.
- Your own example: ____

____

____

❒ **Magical thinking:** You assume a cause-and-effect relationship between two unrelated things even though there is no logical connection between them. It's often based in a belief that certain things can control or impact unrelated events, like someone's fate or misfortune. Superstitions are one form of magical thinking.

Examples:

- "I failed the exam because I didn't have my lucky pencil."
- You think you must knock on wood to prevent something bad from happening.
- Your own example: ____

____

____

❐ **Thought-action fusion:** You believe that if you think about something, it makes it more likely to actually happen.

Examples:

- Because you thought about screaming out a curse word in class, you think it means you are more likely to do it.
- "I had the thought about stealing a toy from the store, so it must mean I'm a bad person, and that any day now, I won't be able to hold back any longer and will end up stealing something on impulse."
- Your own example: ____

____

____

❐ **Emotional reasoning:** You treat your feelings as facts. You assume that if you feel something, it must be true.

Examples:

- You feel scared, so you believe it must be a sign that something bad is going to happen.
- "I feel stupid, so I must be stupid."
- Your own example: ____

____

____

❒ **Magnifying:** You exaggerate the importance of something small or blow negative events out of proportion.

Examples:

- Your report card isn't as good as you hoped it would be, and you tell yourself, "I'm never going to do well in school or get a good job. What's the point of trying? I should just drop out."
- "I forgot my line and *everyone* was staring at me."
- Your own example: ____

____

____

❒ **Minimizing:** You lessen the importance of a success or an achievement.

Examples:

- You believe you only got the award because your teacher felt sorry for you.
- "I only did well on the test because it was easy."
- Your own example: ____

____

____

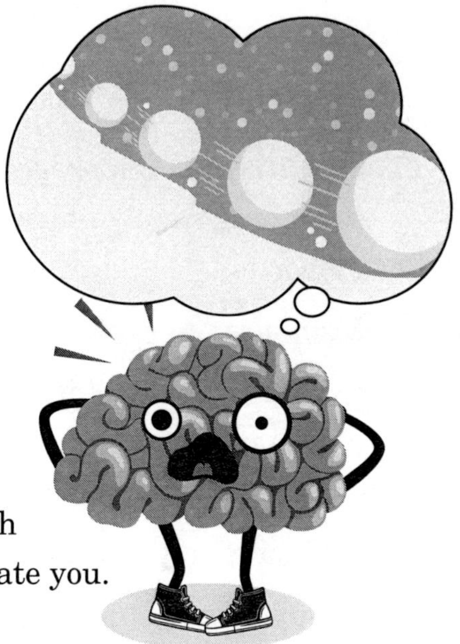

- ❐ **Snowballing:** You exaggerate an initial worry or single event into a pattern of constant defeat. One thing leads to a series of escalating thoughts that cause you to arrive at a general conclusion.

  Examples:

  - Because your classmate didn't want to go out with you, you believe no one is ever going to want to date you. You assume you are going to end up alone.
  - "If I make a mistake, my teachers won't think I'm smart. If they don't think I'm smart, I'll lose their respect. If I lose their respect, they won't write me a letter of recommendation for college, and I'll never be successful."
  - Your own example: ______________________________

    ____

    ____

- ❐ **"I can't handle it":** You believe that you won't be able to cope with something anxiety-provoking or challenging. You underestimate your ability to deal with difficult things.

  Examples:

  - You assume that if you face your fear, you'll be so anxious that you won't be able to manage it.
  - "I can't handle the feeling of being dirty."
  - Your own example: ______________________________

    ____

    ____

"My OCD told me that my teacher was disappointed in me because I didn't get 100 on my science test. I realized this was a *mind-reading* thinking trap."

—ELIANA, AGE 12

"My OCD always told me that something bad was going to happen to my family if I didn't say my prayers exactly right every night before bed. I realized that I was falling into *magical thinking* and *perfectionism* thinking traps."

—JACKSON, AGE 10

SUMMARY

Now that you've reviewed some of the most common thinking traps, did you notice any in your thinking? Some people go through this list and identify a few traps that they've experienced, while others find that *many* of these traps relate to them. There were several that I related to for sure! Rest assured that if you do find yourself falling into thinking traps like these, there *are* ways to change your thinking. We'll go over how to do this in the next chapter.

CHAPTER 5

Don't Believe Everything You Think!

In the previous chapter, you learned about different thinking traps that may come up if you have a *tricky, sticky, picky* brain. This is important because if you learn to spot the thinking traps that keep picking on you, you'll be better equipped to fight back against OCD. One of the ways to do this is by identifying and challenging your unhelpful thoughts with a skill called *cognitive restructuring*.

What exactly does this mean? Well, we all have a *lot* of different thoughts. Some of these are thoughts we should pay attention to, while others are thoughts we should ignore because they don't make much sense. They might be super silly thoughts that we should just laugh at, or extra worrisome, upsetting, or scary thoughts that aren't likely or realistic. Since thoughts can be *tricky*, it's often difficult to know whether or not we should take a thought seriously or ignore it. Since thoughts can also be *sticky*, it can be tough to get our minds off them as well. Cognitive restructuring is a skill that can help you figure out what to do when you have these thoughts, such as whether to pay attention to them or ignore them. It's a skill that helps you learn not to believe everything you think!

Cognitive restructuring involves four basic steps:

1. **Recognize the thoughts you are having. These are often thoughts that lead you to feel anxious or upset.**

2. **Identify any thinking traps.**

3. **Check the facts to see if your thought makes sense.**

4. **Come up with a new, balanced thought that makes more sense.**

We've already covered the first two steps in previous chapters—recognizing your thoughts (step 1) and identifying your thinking traps (step 2). In this chapter, you'll learn how to check the facts and ask questions to see if your thoughts make sense (step 3) and come up with a new, balanced thought that makes more sense (step 4).

Check the Facts

Let's talk about why it isn't a good idea to believe everything you think. Sometimes the thoughts you have aren't based on actual facts; they're just based on your personal opinion or feelings instead of the truth. That's why you have to do some investigative work in these situations and put on your detective hat. When you act like a detective, you look for evidence that tells you whether your thoughts are likely to be realistic or true, or whether they're likely to be unrealistic or false.

What exactly is *evidence*? In a court of law, evidence refers to clear and overwhelming proof that something did (or did not) happen. For example, if someone is suspected of stealing a bunch of cakes from a bakery, we'd look for evidence to give us clues about whether or not they actually did it. This evidence might include finding their fingerprints inside the bakery, catching them with icing all over their mouth, seeing video footage of them committing the crime, or finding the stolen cakes in their possession. If we only had a *feeling* that they committed the crime, that wouldn't be enough evidence to pass in a court of law. We would need actual facts or evidence to hold them accountable for the crime.

IMPORTANT POINT

A feeling is not evidence. Just because you feel worried or scared, it doesn't mean that there is any real reason to be worried or scared. *Feelings aren't facts!* Likewise, just thinking or feeling that something bad may happen does not mean it will actually happen.

I want you to apply the same definition of evidence when you are examining your thoughts. Similar to the cake thief example, think of yourself as an investigator looking for clues to figure out whether your thoughts make sense or if you are perhaps thinking about things in unhelpful ways. For example, if you have a thought that something bad is going to happen, you want to search for clues to decide whether or not to take the thought seriously.

To help with this process, you can ask yourself the following questions:

LIST OF QUESTIONS TO CHECK THE FACTS!

- What is the evidence or "proof" that *supports* this thought?
- What is the evidence or "proof" that *does not* support this thought?
- What is the probability or likelihood that your worry or fear will come true?
- Has this happened before? How many times?
- If it has happened before, what's the chance that it will happen again?
- Are you sure that something bad will happen?
- Are you being overly negative or expecting the worst?
- What would someone else think about this situation?
- What would be the worst-case scenario? Would you be able to deal with it? If it did happen, could you figure out a way to move forward?
- What is probably going to happen?
- What are the pros and cons of thinking this way?

Let's go through some examples of what this might look like. We'll first explain this skill with a thought that might seem a little silly.

Situation	You're lying in bed at night and having difficulty falling asleep.
Thought(s)	"Aliens are going to come down from outer space, kidnap me, and take me to their UFO. I should stay awake, just in case." "Hmm . . . what a weird thought. Maybe it's a sign? Maybe it's a warning that this is actually going to happen!"
Feeling(s)	Scared, anxious, curious
Thinking Trap(s)	Overimportance of thoughts, thought-action fusion

Check the Facts!	What is the evidence or "proof" that *supports* this thought? "There isn't any evidence that I can think of." What's the evidence or "proof" that *does not* support this thought? "I've never actually seen an alien myself, so I can't be sure that they even exist." Has this happened before? How many times? "No, this has never happened. I have never been kidnapped by aliens. I also don't know anyone else who has been kidnapped by aliens." What would someone else think about this situation? "They'd probably say it's a silly thought, and that I just have a big imagination. They probably wouldn't give it much attention."

Develop New, Balanced Thoughts

Once you've checked the facts, you will probably realize that your worries are unlikely to come true, or at least less likely than you initially thought. You can then choose to ignore the thought or develop a more balanced way of thinking about the situation that takes the evidence into account. Remember, "what-if" thoughts are *not* evidence. A "chance" of something bad happening is *not* evidence. A "feeling" that something bad could happen is *not* evidence. Rather, evidence refers to clear and convincing facts that support (or do not support) your thoughts. Cognitive restructuring helps bring this all to light.

Returning to the UFO example, after checking the facts, you'll likely see that there isn't any real good evidence to support the thought that aliens are going to come kidnap you and take you to outer space. Given that you don't have good evidence to support that fear, you would then engage in step 4 of cognitive restructuring, which is to come up with a more balanced thought that takes into account all the evidence that you've considered.

New, More Balanced Thought	"There is no evidence that aliens will kidnap me and take me back to their UFO, so this is likely just my imagination. I bet I'll be safe if I go to sleep."

We mentioned someone previously who has a fear of dogs. Now let's look at an example of cognitive restructuring with that fear in mind.

Situation	Someone with a fear of dogs sees a small dog on a leash with its owner. The dog is playfully wagging its tail.
Thought(s)	"I'm in danger." "It's going to bite me."
Feeling(s)	Nervous, threatened
Thinking Trap(s)	Catastrophizing, fortune-telling
Check the Facts!	What is the evidence or "proof" that *supports* this thought? "There isn't any evidence that the dog is going to hurt me. It isn't barking, growling, or snarling its teeth. In fact, it isn't doing anything aggressive at all." What is the evidence or "proof" that *does not* support this thought? "It's wagging its tail and rolling over to let people rub its belly. That seems to suggest that the dog is friendly and safe to be around, rather than aggressive." Has this happened before? How many times? "I've never really been bitten by a dog, other than a time when a cute puppy was nipping at me when we were playing. Never anything that actually hurt." What is probably going to happen? "It's probably pretty unlikely that this dog will hurt me. It's also on a leash, and the owner seems to have control of it."

After thinking through these questions, you may see that there isn't good evidence to support the fear that you are in danger because of the dog. In fact, you may realize that there is evidence that does *not* support the fear. Now you can come up with a more balanced thought that takes into account all the evidence in this situation.

New, More Balanced Thought	"This dog seems very friendly. The owner also seems to have control of it. It's probably not going to hurt me, so I bet it's safe for me to be nearby."

Here's an example of a situation when someone's OCD tries to pick on them when they are studying for a test.

Situation	A student is preparing for an upcoming test at school.
Thought(s)	"If I don't complete my study routine exactly right, I'm going to fail this test, and then I won't get into college."
Feeling(s)	Anxious, overwhelmed
Thinking Trap(s)	All-or-nothing thinking, jumping to conclusions, fortune-telling, catastrophizing
Check the Facts!	What is the evidence or "proof" that *supports* this thought? "I've never heard of one test (or even one class) being the reason that someone didn't get into college. College acceptances take into account years of grades from many classes, not just one test." What is the evidence or "proof" that *does not* support the thought? "I haven't always had this study routine, and I've never failed a test before, so it's possible that my *tricky, sticky, picky* brain is trying to trick me into doing a study routine that isn't really necessary." What would be the worst-case scenario? Would you be able to deal with it? "If I did fail this test, it probably wouldn't make much of an impact. It's just one grade, and my other grades are really good. I could handle it even if I failed." What are the pros and cons of thinking this way? "There aren't any pros of thinking that I must follow a specific study routine in order to do well on a test." "The cons are that I would be making a decision based on what-if thoughts instead of facts, and if I give my what-if thoughts too much attention, it'll probably just make my anxiety stronger over time."

After reviewing the evidence, it's pretty clear that this person was expecting the worst to happen if they didn't listen to their OCD, when there really isn't any good reason to think it would actually occur. Here's a more balanced thought that takes into account all the facts.

New, More Balanced Thought	"I've felt nervous for tests before and still done well, even without completing my study routine. I'm probably going to do just fine on this test too. I'll try my best, and I'll be able to deal with whatever grade I get."

Test Your Knowledge!

Based on what you've learned so far, take your best guess about which of the following thoughts are *tricky, sticky, picky* thoughts that you should ignore and which are more balanced, realistic thoughts that might make sense. You can find an answer key at the end of this chapter.

	***Tricky, Sticky, Picky* Thought**	**Realistic Thought**
1. My parents will forget to pick me up from school, and I'll end up alone all night locked inside the school.		
2. It might rain today.		
3. I can't go to sleep unless everything in my room is "just right."		
4. If I don't knock on wood three times, something bad will happen.		
5. I could get sick if my friend coughs and sneezes on me over and over.		
6. If I think about it enough, my favorite movie star will show up at my house for dinner tonight.		
7. I might not like the casserole that Grandma made for dinner.		
8. If I think about winning the lottery, it will surely happen.		

	Tricky, Sticky, Picky Thought	Realistic Thought
9. It's possible that my nervousness will make it difficult for me to fall asleep at night.		
10. If I'm late to school, my teacher could be disappointed.		
11. My teeth are going to fall out unless I brush and floss perfectly, every morning and every night.		
12. I'm going to be horrible if I try a new sport.		
13. My stomachache must mean that something is seriously wrong with me.		
14. The principal walked by without saying hello to me. She must think I'm a bad kid.		
15. It's helpful to keep things organized.		
16. I didn't say my prayers perfectly. I'm going to go to hell.		
17. When I sit down to take the test, I'm going to forget everything I studied.		
18. I should probably wash my hands after handling a toxic chemical.		
19. If I think about saying a bad word, I'm probably going to do it.		
20. I can't handle things if they aren't done my way.		

IMPORTANT POINT

This quiz is included to help you get better at recognizing when thoughts may be based in OCD versus when they are more realistic. However, it isn't always obvious which thoughts are based in OCD since *any* thought can become obsessive. That's why you consider the evidence to help you take your "best guess" about whether to take the thought seriously or treat it as OCD.

Now that you've gone through several examples, use the worksheet on the next page to go through an example of one of your own *tricky, sticky, picky* thoughts. To set the stage for this, it's important to recall the thought-feeling-behavior cycle that we introduced in chapter 3, which shows how our thoughts, feelings, and behaviors are all related to each other. After you identify the situation and your thoughts about it, write down whatever feelings you have. (Note: It may be more than one.) For example, are you worried, nervous, or scared? Or maybe confused, sad, or frustrated?

Then, rate how intense or distressing those feelings are using a SUD scale (where 0 is "no distress at all" and 10 is "the most distress you could possibly experience"). That will help you "take the temperature" of how much the thought is bothering you. For example, maybe you are feeling scared, but you only feel a little scared, so you rate that as a 3. Or perhaps you feel completely terrified, marked by shaking and crying, so you rate that as a 9. More intense feelings can often be more difficult to manage.

Next, identify any thinking traps you can recognize in your thoughts. Then check the facts and come up with a more balanced thought. Once you've done that, rerate the intensity of the feelings you first identified to see if they have changed at all. You'll often find that cognitive restructuring can make distressing emotions feel less intense. For example, if your SUD level was initially a 9 because you feared that you were in serious danger, perhaps it decreases to a 4 once you realize that you aren't in such danger.

"I never used to question what my OCD was telling me. I now know that it lies to me, so I shouldn't always believe what it says."

—MALIK, AGE 10

Challenging *Tricky, Sticky, Picky* Thoughts

Situation

Thought(s)

Feeling(s)
(SUD level: 0–10)

Thinking Trap(s)

Check the Facts!

New, More Balanced Thought
(Refer to the "Check the Facts" questions on page 53 to help with challenging anxious thoughts.)

Feeling(s)
(Rerate your SUD level after completing this worksheet.)

Well, how did it go? You can use that worksheet anytime you have a *tricky, sticky, picky* thought that makes you feel worried or upset. The hope is that you'll feel less anxious or distressed after completing the worksheet, as it will help you think about things in more balanced ways. If you do feel less anxious or distressed, you'll probably be more willing to push back against OCD, and that is the ultimate goal! Just know that this skill does take some practice, but in time, you may even be able to go through these steps in your head. I'm at the point now where I can do it on the fly!

Hopefully, this chapter has shown you that although you can't control what thoughts pop into your head, you *can* control what you do about them! Some thoughts are just like spam emails or text messages: You may not be able to stop receiving them completely, but you can learn which ones to disregard when they do pop up. That's what cognitive restructuring will help you do.

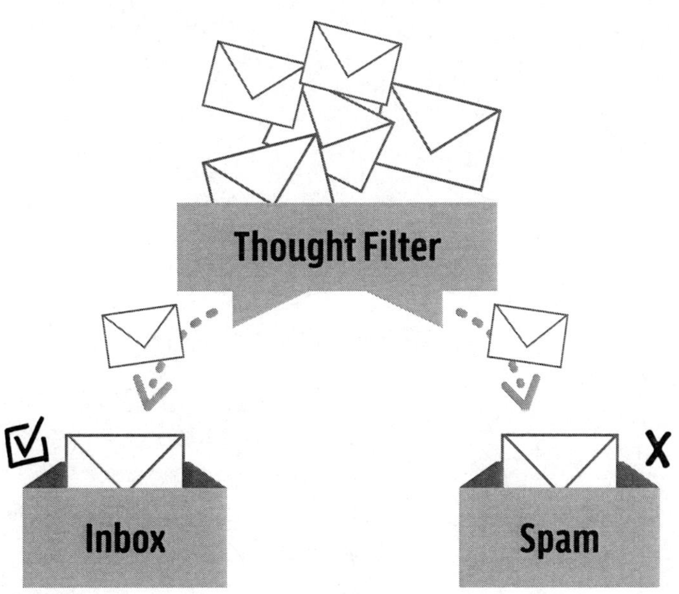

"Okay, this whole 'checking the facts' thing makes sense, but I've tried to use logic to fight back against my OCD thoughts. My family also tries to tell me to 'think rationally,' but that doesn't always work. What do I do then?"

—SPENCER, AGE 11

Spencer brings up a good point that is important to highlight with OCD, which is this: It's rarely enough to *just* challenge your thoughts. Even if you realize that your fears are unlikely to come true, OCD may still cause you to get stuck on the *possibility* that something bad could happen. A *tricky, sticky, picky* brain doesn't want to accept even the smallest chance that a fear could come true. As a result, you might feel like you still need to do what the OCD wants "just in case." That means that although cognitive restructuring is a helpful skill to gain control over OCD, it's not the only one.

Instead, cognitive restructuring works best when it's used *in combination with* a treatment known as exposure and response prevention (ERP), in which you face your fears head-on and keep yourself from doing whatever OCD tells you to do. Basically, while cognitive restructuring is about changing unhelpful thoughts, ERP is about changing unhelpful behaviors. Cognitive restructuring helps you prepare for ERP because when you have enough evidence to recognize that your concerns are likely based in OCD, you'll hopefully be more willing to take the steps to *change your behavior,* and that is the most important part of gaining control over OCD. In the next chapter, you'll learn more about ERP.

Answer Key: Test Your Knowledge (page 57)

Tricky, sticky, picky thoughts: 1, 3, 4, 6, 8, 11, 13, 14, 16, 17, 19, 20

Realistic thoughts: 2, 5, 7, 9, 10, 12, 15, 18

CHAPTER 6

Changing Your *Tricky, Sticky, Picky* Behavior

The key ingredient to challenging a *tricky, sticky, picky* brain is to change your behavior through a form of cognitive behavioral therapy known as *exposure and response prevention* (ERP). With ERP, you gradually confront the thoughts, images, and situations that trigger your obsessions *without* engaging in compulsions. This is broken down into two main components: (1) exposure, in which you face your fears and do what makes you anxious or uncomfortable, and (2) response prevention, in which you resist doing whatever rituals or compulsions you typically do to feel better.

Exposure: Purposely facing the feared situation, object, or thought that triggers anxiety or discomfort

Response prevention: Refraining from the rituals or compulsions that you typically do to reduce anxiety or feel better

Why does ERP work to combat OCD? To explain this, let's refer back to the OCD cycle, in which your *tricky, sticky, picky* brain tells you to engage in a variety of behaviors (or compulsions) so that you'll feel less anxious, uncomfortable, or worried. Though these behaviors can be annoying, upsetting, and time-consuming, you may do them because:

1. They make you feel less anxious, nervous, or worried.
2. You feel "off" or it feels "wrong" if you don't do them.
3. They help you feel more certain or sure about something.
4. You think they're necessary to keep you, your friends, or your family safe.
5. You think they're necessary to prevent something bad from happening.

6. You think the stress or worry will never go away unless you get the compulsion over with.
7. You feel like you can't handle the discomfort if your feared outcome were to happen.
8. You've always done them, and you don't know what it would be like to not do them.

Since these reasons can be convincing, they often keep you from changing your behavior, so the OCD cycle keeps getting stronger unless you do something to stop it. For example, consider a child who worries about getting sick from contaminated food. This makes them feel anxious, so they constantly examine their food for any indication that it is spoiled, check expiration dates, and ask family members for reassurance that their food is okay to eat.

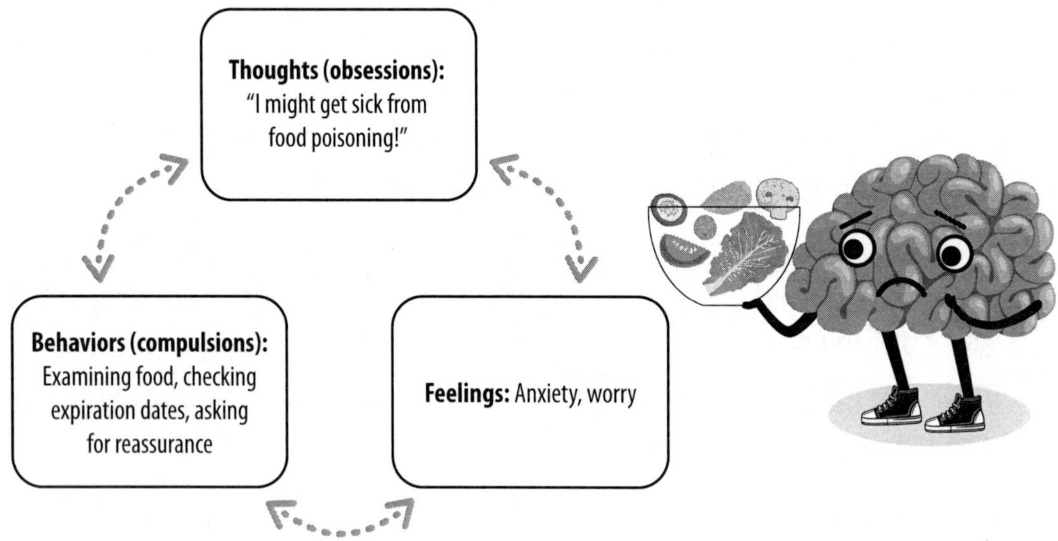

After the child compulsively examines and checks their food and asks others for confirmation, they feel reassured that it is safe, so they go ahead and eat it. If they don't get food poisoning afterward (which is usually the case), they assume that their food-checking compulsions prevented them from getting sick, so the child continues these compulsions over time. This just makes their OCD stronger because they never learn that what they feared would happen was most likely not going to happen (and if it did, that they could deal with it!).

For another example, consider a child who has a thought that they think is immoral or inappropriate (e.g., thoughts of giving their school principal the finger, thoughts of marrying the devil). This makes them feel embarrassed, ashamed, and scared, so they confess the thought to a parent to get reassurance that they are a good kid. After the child gets reassurance, they feel less anxious, and the thought doesn't bother them so much. Unfortunately, the child learns that the confessing and reassurance-seeking helped them feel better, which leads them to confess other thoughts in the future, further strengthening the OCD cycle.

The point is, the longer the OCD cycle continues, the more convinced you become that your compulsions are necessary. You may genuinely believe that your compulsive behaviors are keeping you safe or helping you in some way, so it feels really anxiety-provoking to consider breaking the cycle. This leaves you feeling stuck on an endless path of listening to OCD.

So, how do you break the cycle?

Let's consider this: What do you think would happen if you had an OCD thought and had the urge to do a compulsion to feel better, but you didn't listen to your OCD? That's right. What if you just *didn't* do what your *tricky, sticky, picky* brain wanted you to do? When kids with OCD get asked this question, this is a common response that comes up:

If this is your response, it basically means that your OCD cycle is so strong that you haven't even considered the possibility of responding in a different way! That's okay. We'll work together to overcome your OCD cycle in this chapter.

Some other responses I've gotten from kids are:

. . . And then what would happen?

. . . And then what?

. . . So, do you think your anxiety would just go up and up and just *never* stop? Like, would you explode?

The truth is, many kids with a *tricky, sticky, picky* brain haven't really considered the idea of going against what their brain tells them to do, as it feels way too scary or too risky. Some kids even worry that their anxiety will just keep going up until they either go crazy or explode! (For the record: There haven't been any reports to date of anyone exploding because they've used these strategies.)

I used to have a lot of these concerns when it came to my own OCD, but what if I told you that the process doesn't tend to happen how you may think? Certainly, if you go against what your *tricky, sticky, picky* brain wants, it probably won't like it. It may also be confused at first, as it won't understand why you are doing something different all of a sudden. Though your anxiety will probably increase at first, it won't continue to go up forever. It will eventually come down! It's physically impossible for your body to stay in a state of extreme anxiety forever. The problem is that most people don't wait it out to see what *actually* happens. But if you're willing to tolerate it long enough and *not* give in to your OCD, you'll often find that your anxiety will either start to decrease or at least begin to feel more manageable. It's kind of like a bug bite. If you scratch it, it'll continue to worsen, get bigger, and itch more over time. If you resist the urge to scratch, though it may be extra itchy temporarily, the itch will eventually go away.

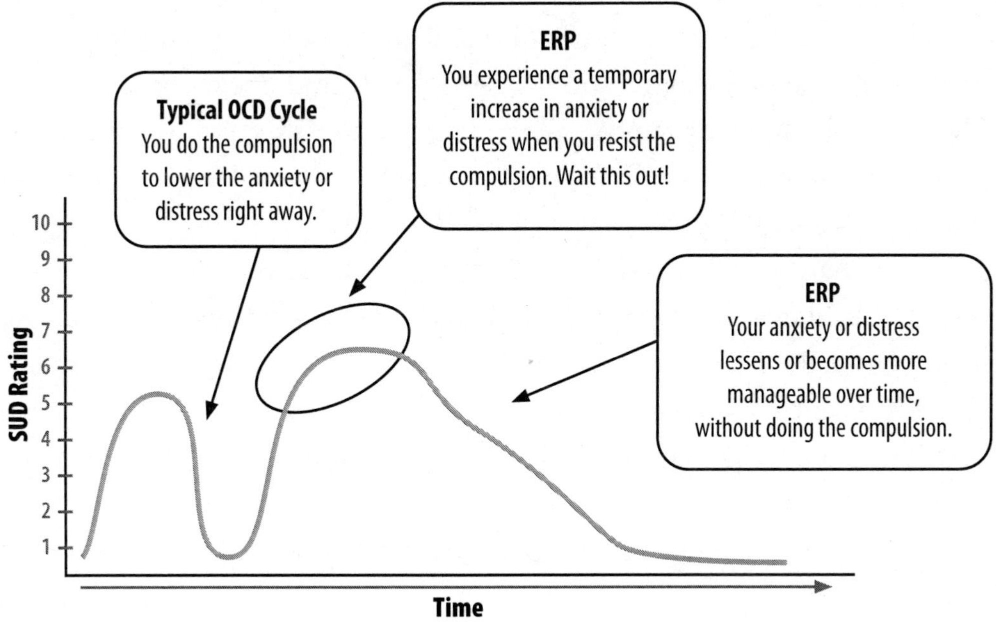

Let's go through an example to show how this may occur. Imagine that you join the swim team and it's your first day. You go to dip your toe in the pool, and it feels really cold, so you quickly jump back. Your automatic urge is to stay out of the pool. You don't, though, because your team is counting on you. So, you put on your swim cap and jump in! Although the water felt pretty cold at first, after you swim around the pool a bit, you eventually get used to the temperature and it doesn't bother you as much. As you continue to tackle the cold pool over and over again each day at swim practice, it gets easier and easier to jump in since you know your body will get used to it. You learn that you can handle it.

You experience something similar if you take on tough things with ERP. When you confront your triggers, you learn that your anxiety or distress lessens over time (which is called *habituation*) or you learn to tolerate your anxiety much better. Not only that, but by doing these repeated exposures or "experiments," you learn a lot more. For example, you often learn that you don't need to be so anxious or fearful, that your feared outcomes are unlikely to happen, and that your worries are not as powerful as you think. Once I experienced this all myself, it was a game changer for me!

Of course, OCD doesn't like it when we don't do what it wants, so it often tries to push back and make a scene to try to get us to give in. But when it realizes that you won't, it tends to back down. Consider this example: You give your dog some food from the dinner table one night. He comes back the next night and the next night looking for food and you drop some food for him. This goes on for several months, until the vet suddenly tells you to chill out on giving your dog table food, as it's not so healthy for him. The first night that you stop, the dog is confused about why he isn't getting food, so he whimpers, cries, and gives you puppy dog eyes. If that doesn't work, he'll probably bark and become even more disruptive to really get your attention. If you still aren't having it, your dog may try begging from other people at the table to see if his antics might work with them.

However, if you all stay firm, your dog will eventually realize that he's just not getting food, and he'll eventually give up and go back to taking his nap. Your dog might still try to beg for food for a few nights after that, but if you refuse to give in, he'll give up more quickly each time and, eventually, he won't try much at all. When you use ERP for the first time, OCD may similarly try to get you to give in by trying all sorts of things to get your attention. If you stay firm though, stick it out, and trust the process, it will back down when it sees that you aren't taking the bait.

Using ERP to Take Reasonable Risks and Overcome Your Fears

Now that you understand how ERP works, let's go through an example of how you could use it to change your *tricky, sticky, picky* behaviors and break the OCD cycle. Let's say you are extremely fearful of germs, and you worry about getting sick or spreading disease if you touch "contaminated" objects (obsession). As a result, you avoid touching door handles because they might have other people's germs on them (compulsion). You do so by using barriers, like paper towels or your shirt, to open doors or by washing your hands excessively if you do touch a door handle.

If you decide that you're fed up with your *tricky, sticky, picky* brain telling you what to do, you can use ERP to change your behavior by touching door handles with your bare hands and *not* washing or sanitizing them after. Although you predict that this will cause you to get sick, you can be open to doing this experiment to see what *actually* happens. You touch a door handle once, and you don't get sick. You then do it again, and you still don't get sick. You do it fifteen more times and still don't get sick. In this case, you are surprised to learn that what *actually* happened was very different from what you *expected* to happen. You learn that you can touch doorknobs and be okay, which reduces the strength of your old belief: "I'll get sick if I touch doorknobs."

At this point, you might be wondering what happens if you actually *do* get sick. In other words, what if you start touching door handles all the time, and on the twentieth time, you get sick? Would that teach you that you shouldn't touch door handles? Good question! One of the ways that OCD often wins is because of the argument that "There's always a chance that something could go wrong, so you better not risk it." However, it is truly impossible to eliminate all risk in life, and if you tried, it would likely lead to a very limited and unsatisfying life. If you give it some thought, I bet you can think of a ton of other risks that you encounter each day that you may not even think about. For example, you may play sports, ride in a car, talk to someone new, answer a question in class, eat food that someone else prepared, or go see a new movie. All of these things have some degree of risk involved, whether that may be a risk of something bad happening (e.g., an injury, an accident) or a risk of being disappointed (e.g., disliking food, feeling rejected by a peer, not enjoying a movie that you paid to see). However, OCD has a way of picking and choosing so that it only focuses on *some* risks while being seemingly unbothered by others. This is a reminder of how OCD often doesn't make much sense.

Therefore, it can be a great learning experience if your feared outcome actually *does* happen. This may seem absurd to think about, but it's true! When your feared outcome comes true, you often discover that things aren't as bad as you thought they'd be, and you also learn that you can tolerate things much better than you thought you could. For example, if you get a cold after touching a doorknob, you learn that it's unpleasant, but you can get through it. A phrase I've always liked is "Most things are figureoutable" ☻. By accepting a small, reasonable amount of risk, you are able to live your life more freely without being under the control of OCD.

Exposures to Challenge *Tricky, Sticky, Picky* Behavior

Now that you've got a good idea of how ERP works, let's take a look at some ideas of how to change your behavior so you can push back against your *tricky, sticky, picky* brain. Some of these exposures may seem more challenging while others may seem less difficult. Just remember that what is easier for one person may be more difficult for someone else, so there will naturally be differences in terms of the types of exposures people do. Either way, you'll want to consider the specific situations, tasks, and people that trigger your OCD and incorporate these into your exposure goal list. Whenever you push back at all against what OCD wants, you are making positive strides against it.

As you start doing exposures, it's important that you identify and gradually remove any safety behaviors you might be engaging in. A *safety behavior* is anything extra that you do to help you feel more comfortable in an exposure. It might be something you keep with you "just in case" your fear comes true. For example, if you have a fear of vomiting, you might keep saltine crackers, mints, and a bottle of water with you at all times, just in case you feel nauseous. Perhaps you sit by the exit at a movie theater in case you have to rush to the bathroom. Or if you have a fear that you'll accidentally hurt someone, you might keep your hands in your pockets when you walk by family members or see sharp objects to lessen the chance that you could do something to harm others on impulse.

Many people with a *tricky, sticky, picky* brain have a difficult time handling situations that make them feel nervous, worried, or scared, and these safety behaviors help them feel better in the moment. However, these behaviors maintain OCD over time because you start to feel like you *need* to do these behaviors to be okay in those situations. They also interfere with your ability to learn from the exposure and realize that you can handle challenging things. Therefore, as you begin ERP, you'll want to gradually remove these safety behaviors.

Do the Opposite

Think about what OCD is telling you to do, and then think about what the opposite or reverse of that might be. The following table shows some examples.

What OCD Wants	How to Do the Opposite
Check the locks four times.	Don't check the locks at all.
Ask your parents a question to get reassurance.	Refrain from asking your parents a question to get reassurance and practice tolerating feeling unsure.
Touch or tap things evenly so that your body feels "just right."	Touch or tap things unevenly so that your body purposely feels "wrong."
Cancel out "bad" thoughts by replacing them with "good" thoughts.	Don't replace "bad" thoughts with "good" thoughts and practice tolerating the presence of "bad" thoughts.
Fix your writing so it looks perfect.	Leave your writing as-is so it looks imperfect.

Vary the Intensity

If it feels too difficult to do the opposite of what your OCD says, you can start by doing exposures that feel more manageable and less scary. This is better than not doing any exposures at all! One way to think about this is to consider small changes you can make with exposures to either increase or decrease how challenging they are.

Easier		More Challenging
Wash your hands once with soap.	⟷	Rinse your hands off once with just water.
Use toddler scissors to cut a piece of paper.	⟷	Use a sharp knife to cut an apple.
Mess something up "just a little bit."	⟷	Mess something up "a lot."
Touch the floor with your bare hand.	⟷	Eat a small piece of food off the floor.
Think of a feared word.	⟷	Say the feared word aloud.
Touch something contaminated with one finger.	⟷	Touch something contaminated with your whole hand.
Pet a five-pound puppy.	⟷	Pet a 100-pound German Shepherd.

Change the Setting or Location

Are exposures easier (or more difficult) for you at home, at school, or in public? If so, challenge your OCD in an easier setting to begin with and then move up to a more challenging setting. For instance, if you have a therapist, can you first practice the exposure in their office with them before doing it by yourself at home?

Easier		More Challenging
Purposely put things out of place in your therapist's office.	⟷	Purposely put things out of place at home.
Avoid checking your food for contamination when eating in a fancy restaurant.	⟷	Avoid checking your food for contamination when eating in a fast-food restaurant.
Refrain from schoolwork checking rituals at home.	⟷	Refrain from schoolwork checking rituals in class.

Easier		More Challenging
Go to the mall on a weekday (when it is less crowded).	⟷	Go to the mall on the weekend (when it is more crowded).
Use your brother's bathroom.	⟷	Use a gas station bathroom.
Resist rereading rituals in your easiest class.	⟷	Resist rereading rituals in your hardest class.

Change Who Is Involved and What They Do

If you have OCD, it is super common for your parents, friends, or family members to be involved in your rituals in some way. Maybe they check something for you because it is too time-consuming for you to check it yourself. Maybe you have a nighttime routine that requires them to answer certain questions. Maybe you feel like doing a certain ritual is more or less risky depending on whether someone is there with you. Think about all the ways other people are involved and start gradually decreasing what they do. (Note: You'll learn much more about this in chapter 10.)

Easier		More Challenging
Lock the door once when a parent is nearby.	⟷	Lock the door once when you're alone.
Cut up an apple when you're by yourself.	⟷	Cut up an apple with a sibling nearby.
Have your parent repeat their answer to a question three times.	⟷	Have your parent answer a question only one time.
Ask your parent to thoroughly check your food before you eat it.	⟷	Do not ask your parent to check your food before you eat it.
Limit yourself to five confessions to your parent per day.	⟷	Limit yourself to one confession to your parent per day.
Go #2 in the bathroom. Have your parent present to observe that you wiped well.	⟷	Go #2 in the bathroom. Wipe yourself without your parent nearby to observe that you wiped well.

Vary the Quantity

OCD likes you to do things over and over again so you feel sure that you did them properly, or even that you did them at all. So, if it feels too tough to eliminate the rituals completely, you can push back by gradually reducing how much you do things.

What OCD Wants	How to Vary the Quantity
Use five pumps of soap while washing your hands.	Use two pumps of soap while washing your hands.
Check your homework three times.	Check your homework once.
Repeat your prayers seven times.	Repeat your prayers three times.
Get an unlimited amount of reassurance from your parents each day.	Limit reassurance from your parents to ten times per day.
After going to the bathroom, wipe yourself with as much toilet paper as you think you need to feel clean.	Wipe yourself with a maximum of fifteen squares of toilet paper after going to the bathroom, even if you don't feel fully clean.
Rewrite your letters until it feels "right."	Limit yourself to only rewriting letters once.
Confess to a parent any time you have an intrusive thought.	Limit yourself to five confessions to a parent per day.

Vary the Amount of Time

OCD has a way of taking up a lot of time. It also convinces you to spend even *more* time doing your rituals, as if the time you've already spent isn't good enough. One way to push back is to set a time limit on your rituals, even if it feels difficult. Here's a tip: If you leave the exposure with doubts about whether you did a "good enough" job with the task—for example, perhaps you feel you didn't clean "well" enough—that typically means you are on the right track to fight back against OCD. That's because OCD doesn't want you to feel confident that you've done a good job.

What OCD Wants	How to Vary the Amount of Time
Spend thirty minutes reviewing your math assignment.	Spend ten minutes reviewing your math assignment.
Shower as long as it takes to feel completely clean.	Limit yourself to a thirty-minute shower, even if you don't feel fully clean.
Practice your basketball drills for an hour so you can work toward getting them "perfect."	Practice your basketball drills for fifteen minutes.

What OCD Wants	How to Vary the Amount of Time
Wash your hands right away after you feel contaminated.	Delay washing your hands for five minutes after you feel contaminated.
Do two hours of extra daily prayer to make up for any accidental transgressions.	Do thirty minutes of extra daily prayer to make up for any accidental transgressions.
Spend as long as it takes to organize and arrange your room until it feels "just right."	Spend one hour organizing and arranging your room, and stop even if it doesn't feel "just right."

Change the Way You Do It

OCD can be very *picky* in terms of how it wants you to do things, so you can push back against it by doing things differently. Maybe you mix up the order of your routine or you do it in reverse!

What OCD Wants	How to Do It Differently
Do a specific washing routine in the shower (e.g., washing your hair first, then your face, then your shoulders, followed by your belly, and so on).	Complete your washing routine but wash your body parts in a different order (e.g., washing your face first, followed by belly, hair, and so on).
Check each homework item before you move to the next item.	Check your homework once, but only after you have completed the entire assignment.
Have your parents respond with a very specific phrase when they give you reassurance.	Have your parents slightly alter the phrase they respond with when they give you reassurance.
Make sure text messages use proper spelling, grammar, and punctuation.	Use a slang word or a spelling error in a text message.
Drive your regular route to school every day.	Drive a different route to school.
Put your clothing on from top to bottom (e.g., top, underwear, pants, socks, shoes).	Put your clothing on in a random order (e.g., socks, underwear, top, pants, shoes).

Vary the Time of Day

It's pretty common for OCD to pick on you more at certain times of the day. Some kids have more triggers or rituals at nighttime. For example, they might worry that something bad will happen during the night if they don't complete certain rituals or that they won't be relaxed enough to fall asleep if they don't get everything done "right."

Other kids have more rituals in the morning when they are leaving for school or starting their day. Likewise, you might start by challenging your OCD during an easier time of day and then working your way up to doing the exposure at a more challenging time.

Easier		More Challenging
Limit your prayer rituals in the morning.	⟷	Limit your prayer rituals at bedtime.
Resist reassurance-seeking about your health during the daytime.	⟷	Resist reassurance-seeking about your health at bedtime.
Resist wearing sunscreen in evenings (when sun is not out).	⟷	Resist wearing sunscreen during a fifteen-minute recess in the middle of the day (when sun is more likely to be out).
Refrain from checking the stove in the morning.	⟷	Refrain from checking the stove in the evening.
Talk about a worst-case fear that could happen.	⟷	At 9:11 a.m./p.m., talk about a worst-case fear that could happen.

Vary How You're Feeling

Some kids want to feel relaxed before they tackle exposures, so they try to wait until they feel "right." Other kids try to avoid doing exposures when they feel relaxed because they don't want anything to "rock the boat" or ruin how they're feeling. Since you don't know when your OCD triggers are going to pop up in real life, it's best to practice exposures in a variety of feeling states, including when you are anxious, sick, calm, angry, or tired. This will help you feel less vulnerable to OCD, as life rarely waits for us to "feel right" to put hurdles in our way. Show yourself that you are strong enough to tackle OCD no matter what.

Easier		More Challenging
Resist your morning rituals after a good night's sleep.	⟷	Resist your morning rituals when you didn't sleep well the night before.
Don't reread the same sentence in a book during summer reading.	⟷	Don't reread the same sentence in a book during finals week, when you are feeling stressed.

Easier		More Challenging
Do not neutralize random superstitious thoughts.	←→	Do not neutralize superstitious thoughts when you have a "bad feeling."
Resist touching or tapping rituals.	←→	Resist touching or tapping rituals when you are already feeling anxious.
Read about existential questions.	←→	Read about existential questions after you attend a religious service.

Imagine Your Triggers Before Facing Them in Real Life

Imaginal exposures are a way to begin confronting your fears before you actually face them in real life. This type of exposure can be used as an initial step to help you feel more ready to face your fear for real. Or it can be used to help you face fears that may not be realistic for you to face in real life. You might simply imagine what it's like for your worst-case scenario to happen.

Easier (Imaginal Exposure)		More Challenging (Real Exposure)
Imagine answering a question wrong in class and feeling embarrassed.	←→	Actually answer a tough question in class and take the risk that your answer could be wrong.
Imagine having intrusive thoughts while at church or synagogue.	←→	Go to church or synagogue and do not suppress any intrusive thoughts you have while there.
Imagine forgetting to check the stove and a fire starting in the house.	←→	Don't check the stove before you leave the house.
Write a brief paragraph about your worst-case fear coming true.	←→	Write a lengthy narrative about your worst-case fear coming true, making sure to include thoughts, feelings, and all the scariest aspects of the fear.

Refrain from Mental Compulsions

As you learned in chapter 3, mental compulsions often involve reviewing or analyzing something in your mind with the goal of figuring out something or answering some sort of question so you feel less uncertainty. Therefore, the way to challenge these types of compulsions is to *not* answer the question that OCD is trying to get you to answer. For example, a common mental compulsion is to replay past conversations or situations in your mind to make sure you did or said the "right" thing. In this case, the way to challenge OCD is to *not* replay the conversation or situation. Instead, you lean into the feeling of being unsure about what happened. You learn to tolerate the uncertainty about whether or not you said or did something "wrong." It will probably feel uncomfortable at first to leave your question unanswered, but that is exactly what you need to do to gain control over OCD, and it will get easier over time. It will also help you learn that thoughts are just thoughts and they don't always require action.

Or perhaps you have a taboo or scary thought and feel the urge to push it out of your head or counteract it in some way. The way to challenge OCD in this case is to simply allow the presence of the thought without doing anything about it. How do you do this? Consider this analogy. You attend a party and see someone you dislike. You don't need to go up to them and make a scene (this would be like giving too much attention to the OCD), and you also don't need to leave the party altogether to get away from them (this would be like avoiding the OCD). You can just stay at the party without interacting or engaging with them. You just accept their presence and enjoy the rest of the party. You can do the same with a taboo thought by letting it be there while you carry on with whatever else you're doing.

Some kids don't realize that they are engaging in mental compulsions until they have already begun doing them—it feels as if they occur automatically. Just know that if that happens, you can disrupt them at any time. It's as if you start solving a lengthy math problem in your head (10 + 4 – 7 + 15 – 9 + 3 – 6), but you stop solving it halfway through so you don't allow yourself to determine the final answer. Once you realize that you're doing a mental compulsion, just discontinue your effort to get to whatever final answer OCD wants you to get to.

What OCD Wants	How to Challenge Mental Compulsions
Replay a conversation in your head to make sure you didn't offend someone.	Tell yourself, "It's possible that I said something weird or inappropriate, but I'm not going to try to figure it out."
Try to recall your step-by-step movements upon leaving your house (e.g., recollect mental images of turning off the lights and faucets) to be sure that you did everything.	Refrain from recalling your movements upon leaving your house. Allow yourself to experience the feeling of doubt about whether or not you did these things.

What OCD Wants	How to Challenge Mental Compulsions
Think through all the rational reasons why you aren't at risk of doing something dangerous, to reassure yourself that you can let an obsession go.	Tell yourself, "It's possible that I could do something bad or dangerous" instead of convincing yourself that you won't.
Neutralize any "bad" or "inappropriate" thoughts by counteracting them with a "positive" thought.	Let "bad" or "inappropriate" thoughts be present without counteracting them with a "positive" thought—allow the feeling of discomfort to be there.
Rehearse and plan out in detail how you'll handle a future situation.	Deal with the situation in real time rather than planning for it ahead of time; essentially, "just wing it."
Purposely think unwanted or taboo thoughts as a way to "test" how you feel about them (e.g., "Do I like this thought?"; "Am I grossed out by this thought?").	Refrain from analyzing your thoughts or your emotional reactions to thoughts; just tolerate the uncertainty of being unsure how you feel.

IMPORTANT POINT

Mental compulsions often relate to the thinking traps of "overimportance of thoughts" and "need to control thoughts," which we discussed in chapter 4. Remember: Just because you accept the presence of intrusive thoughts *does not* mean that you agree with the thoughts. OCD thoughts *want* you to react to them. Therefore, OCD loses its power if you *don't* react to them. It's just like a bully who makes obnoxious comments to try to get a reaction from you. If you don't engage with the bully or feed into what they're doing, the bully will lose their power and eventually stop picking on you so much. OCD works just like that. You can accept the presence of a thought without giving it further attention or energy.

Spoil the Compulsion

Sometimes compulsions happen so fast that you might find yourself doing them without even realizing it. If you realize you are in the middle of a compulsion, consider whether there may be a way to "spoil" it. Doing this helps you end with a win instead of letting OCD get the last word. Perhaps you counted in your head to end on a certain number (compulsion), so you spoil it by purposely counting further to a number that OCD doesn't like. Maybe you counteracted a "bad" thought with a "good" thought (compulsion), so you spoil the compulsion by purposely thinking a "bad" thought again.

What OCD Had You Do	How to Spoil It
You touched things with your left and right hands to make them feel "even" or "symmetrical."	Purposely touch those things again with just one hand so that you leave it feeling "uneven" or "asymmetrical."
You washed your hands excessively to feel perfectly clean.	Purposely touch something germy to reintroduce a feeling of contamination.
You put your clothing on in a particular order.	Purposely take off a random clothing item and put it back on so it feels out of order.
You took a specific path when you walked from your bedroom to the kitchen.	Purposely go back to your bedroom so you can walk a different way to the kitchen.
You took a mental image of the door lock to feel sure that you locked it.	Glance back at the door lock while distracted to purposely corrupt the mental image that you had in your mind.

Putting It All Together

Now that you have a sense of the many different ways you can challenge OCD, it's time to create a game plan by making a list of exposure challenges that you can work through. We call this list of challenges an *exposure hierarchy*. This hierarchy is just a list of exposure ideas ranked in order of how much distress you think they would cause you (where 0 = "no distress at all" and 10 = "the most distress you could possibly experience"), using the SUD scale we reviewed in earlier chapters. The idea is that you start with lower-level (or easier) challenges first since they often feel less intimidating to tackle. Once you build your confidence with these lower-level challenges, the higher-level (or more challenging) exposures won't feel as scary.

Once you get the hang of using an exposure hierarchy, you can mix it up by going through the list randomly and doing exposures out of order. Or you might prefer to start with exposures that challenge whatever OCD symptoms are causing the most problems for you. Remember, it doesn't matter exactly how you do it, as long as you do it! Though this process might seem intimidating at first, most kids find that it quickly boosts their confidence once they start making positive strides and see the results of their hard work. In this section, I'll provide you with several examples of the challenges that could be on exposure hierarchies for different symptoms of OCD, followed by a blank template for you to create your own.

Perfectionism and "Just-Right" Symptoms	
Exposure	**SUD Rating (0–10)**
Turn in your homework without checking it at all.	9
Touch things unevenly (with only your left hand and not your right hand).	7
Turn in a writing assignment that looks messy.	6
Leave dresser drawers partially open when leaving for school.	5
Check your homework just one time before turning it in.	4
Limit yourself to two minutes to do your hair, even if it isn't "just right."	3
Send a text message without rereading it first.	2

Worries About Causing Harm and Bad Things Happening	
Exposure	**SUD Rating (0–10)**
Resist knocking on wood after having a bad thought about your parents.	8
Resist knocking on wood after having a bad thought about your dog.	7
Refrain from doing your nighttime ritual (e.g., repeating a specific phrase out loud six times) to keep your family safe.	6
Use scissors when your little brother is nearby.	5
Use a pencil when a family member is nearby.	4
Resist knocking on wood after having a bad thought about a friend at school.	3

Concerns About Germs and Contamination	
Exposure	**SUD Rating (0–10)**
Eat food without examining it.	10
Sleep in your bed without taking a nighttime shower.	9
Sleep in your bed after only rinsing off with water in the shower (no soap).	8
Drink milk or eat yogurt without checking the expiration date.	7
Use a disinfectant wipe on the counter; rinse after with water (no soap).	6
Skip washing your legs when you take a shower.	5
Skip washing your feet when you take a shower.	4
Eat bread without checking the expiration date.	3
Eat crackers without checking the expiration date.	2

Your Exposure Hierarchy

Exposure	SUD Rating (0–10)

SUMMARY

In this chapter, we discussed how confronting your fears and challenging your rituals can help you break the cycle of OCD and live life more fully. By doing ERP, you can learn to be in the presence of obsessions—letting them be there for as long as they want—without trying to push them away or giving into your compulsions. That is what allows you to stay focused on moving forward with whatever is important to you. In the next chapter, we'll discuss some common doubts and barriers to OCD treatment that might try to psych you out and get you off course. By becoming familiar with these barriers, you'll be better able to push through them when they pop up.

CHAPTER 7

Doubts and Barriers That Might Show Up

By now, you've identified the many ways that OCD can cause problems for you, and you've also learned how ERP can help you challenge OCD and take back control of your life. Unfortunately, OCD doesn't want you to win, so it will often try to psych you out with various doubts and barriers that get in the way of your willingness to challenge it. OCD is *tricky* that way. Here are some common roadblocks that you might experience when you think about starting treatment:

- Worry that treatment will be too difficult or take up too much time
- Belief that it is easier to just avoid dealing with it
- Fear of what life will be like if OCD is gone
- Worry that treatment will change your personality
- Concern that treatment won't work
- Uncertainty about whether challenging your OCD is important enough
- Worry about the discomfort treatment will cause in the short term instead of considering the long term or the "big picture"
- Belief that OCD is "not that big of a problem"
- Belief that compulsions actually keep you safe or prevent bad things from happening
- Uncertainty of how or where to start
- Lack of people or sources who can support you

If any of these roadblocks are getting in your way, you're not alone. These are common roadblocks that many kids have! Although it's normal to have some skepticism about using the strategies in this book, it's important to not let that skepticism stop you from getting better and breaking free from the cycle of OCD. In this chapter, I'll explore some of the most common doubts and barriers that kids have and discuss how you can overcome them.

Doubts That Interfere with Starting Treatment

"My OCD is different."

A lot of kids feel that their OCD is "different." They think that no one will understand it and that no one has ever struggled with the same kinds of thoughts, worries, and behaviors. Unfortunately, this makes a lot of kids nervous to talk about what bothers them, as they worry that they'll feel embarrassed or judged, be labeled as "weird" or "crazy," or get in trouble in some way. Although you are probably very special in many ways (maybe you have an awesome hidden talent!), your OCD is probably not as special or different as you think. There are thousands of people with a *tricky, sticky, picky* brain just like yours all over the world. While you don't know them, you probably have similar OCD symptoms, so don't let your concerns about "being different" or beliefs that "no one can help you" interfere with your willingness to talk about it and get help.

Still don't buy it? Some kids don't at first. However, if you read about some of my friends with OCD (coming up in chapter 12) and learn about all the ways that it picks on people, you'll probably realize that what I'm saying is true. You may think, "Wow, that sounds just like me! I do that too!" So keep an open mind, give it a chance, and I bet you'll see that you can get help too, just like I did.

"Okay . . . so it might work, but what if it doesn't? What if I'm the one person it doesn't work for?"

Kids often worry that they will be the *one* kid whom these strategies don't work for, even if they work for others. While that is certainly possible, it is pretty unlikely. In fact, the vast majority of people who use these strategies get better! It's for that reason that ERP is considered the "gold standard" of treatment for OCD—meaning it's the most effective. If, for some reason, these strategies don't seem to work for you, you can always reach out to a therapist who specializes in OCD to brainstorm and problem-solve whether anything may be getting in your way. For example, maybe you're engaging in subtle rituals, safety behaviors, or mental compulsions that are interfering with your learning without you realizing it. Or maybe you'd benefit from incorporating other science-based methods into your efforts, like skills that enhance emotion regulation, improve attention or focus, or build motivation. So, I encourage you to give these treatment strategies a try and put yourself up to the challenge.

"What if it makes me worse?"

OCD is very convincing in making you believe that you have to follow its rules if you want to be okay. It's kind of *tricky* in that way. However, remember that thousands of kids and adults have used the strategies in this book and found them to work incredibly well. There are also tons of scientific studies that show how effective ERP is. Given that, there's good reason to believe that these tools can help you too. So, if you're nervous that they will make you worse, the best thing to do is to start with small, less difficult challenges. Once you build some confidence and see that these tools work, it will be easier for you to take bigger and bigger steps to challenge OCD. Although it may feel like you are taking a big risk to fight against OCD, it is a risk that is well worth it!

"Talking about my problems will just make them worse."

Some kids worry that if they talk about their OCD, they'll start thinking about their symptoms more often, which will make them feel worse. This is just another *tricky* way that OCD tries to trick you into not fighting back. Sure, it's possible that your symptoms may *temporarily* worsen once OCD gets the clue that you are starting to challenge it, but it's also possible that this won't happen. In fact, some people feel better really early on in treatment because it's a relief to finally talk about something that has been troubling them for so long.

The other option is to not deal with your symptoms, in which case you'll probably continue to be under the control of OCD for a long time. If you consider the big picture, would you rather have a brief period of increased anxiety (but in a way that ultimately helps you feel much better), or would you rather do nothing and have OCD continue to pick on you for a very long time? This ended up being a pretty easy decision for me, as I was eager to stop the endless cycle of OCD from picking on me, day after day.

"My OCD isn't really a problem" or "It's not that bad."

If you don't think that your OCD is a problem, I understand why you might not be too motivated to put in the time and effort to work on it. However, let's consider whether you might be minimizing how much OCD really impacts your life. Do you change your behavior or avoid things because of OCD? Do other people change their behavior because of your OCD? Think about a typical day for you, from the time you wake up until the time you go to bed, and consider when OCD interferes with your day. For example, do you have to spend excess time doing rituals before leaving the house? Or when getting dressed? Or before eating?

Or perhaps you don't think OCD is a problem because your family does a lot of things for you, such as taking over chores or handling contaminated items for you, that might otherwise trigger your OCD. Maybe they even participate in some of your rituals with you, like checking things over or giving you reassurance a certain number of times. If you were to eliminate all of the ways that your family changes their behavior to work around your OCD, what would that be like for you? If the answer is "difficult," then there's a good chance that your OCD is making more of an impact than you think.

Another thing to consider is whether the way you currently handle OCD will work long term. One day, you might want to attend college, get a job, get married, move to a different city, or live somewhere without your parents. You probably won't bring your parents to college, to a job, or on a date. Maybe they do a lot for you now, but they will probably be less involved in the future. The sooner you work on your OCD, the sooner you'll get to the other side and have more confidence that you can handle these new situations more independently.

"I'll just stop one day" or "I'll grow out of it."

OCD is not just a phase. It is a very real disorder that is likely to stay a part of your life unless you manage it. As we discussed in chapter 1, science has shown that there are differences in how the brain works in people with OCD versus those without it, so it isn't likely to go away on its own. Instead, there's a good chance it will get worse if left untreated. It often does this in very subtle ways, so you may not notice it happening at first. For example, OCD might want you to do "just one more" check, which ultimately leads to more and more checks. Before long, it's picking on you in a variety of new ways. Given that, it's best to challenge it sooner rather than later, before it gets any worse. It's a lot easier to overcome a small problem versus a larger one.

"I tried treatment before, and it didn't work."

Unfortunately, some kids have had previous experiences with therapy that weren't so helpful, so they understandably think that the strategies in this book won't help either. If this has been your experience, I want to acknowledge what a major disappointment that is. It makes sense that you'd feel discouraged and frustrated. However, it's possible that you worked with a therapist who didn't understand OCD very well or who wasn't very experienced in ERP. Not every therapist is an expert in OCD, just like not every teacher is an expert in every subject. Or perhaps the therapist just wasn't a good fit for you. I'm sorry if this happened to you, but don't let these past experiences cause you to give up on the idea that you can get better—because you can.

"I don't know what life is like without OCD."

Some kids are so wrapped up in their OCD that they almost feel like it defines them. I get it—familiarity can be comfortable. You might be nervous to get rid of what you know for something you don't know. Your OCD might also provide you with a feeling of safety or control. However, just realize that these are *false* feelings of safety, and they do not compare to the confidence you will gain when you know how to push back against OCD! I've also never heard of anyone who has overcome OCD and said, "I really wish I could go back to doing all those rituals." If anything, kids tend to wish that they worked on it sooner. In addition, while OCD may be a part of you, there is so much more to you than just your OCD, like the fact that you might be a good friend, an awesome piano player, a talented cook, or a leader who advocates for your peers. It is important to get OCD under control so you can let those other things shine through.

"I believe my OCD."

Some kids do not want to challenge their OCD because they believe that it protects them or keeps them safe. Maybe you think it's a special, unique quality that you have, as if you have the power and responsibility to keep bad things from happening—perhaps even that you're the "chosen one"—because you have this characteristic. Maybe you think that it's God's way of protecting you or testing you, so you should listen. Or perhaps you don't think your worries are excessive or irrational, and you think your rituals make sense, so you aren't willing to push back against them. If your doubts are based in any of these beliefs, I encourage you to learn even more about OCD and focus on its actual impact on your life and well-being. The next chapter will help you reflect on the ways OCD has affected your life so you can make a thoughtful decision about whether or not to keep listening to OCD.

"I'm not ready to work on it."

Maybe you don't feel ready to work on your OCD. Maybe your parents or other family members are pushing you to work on it, but you're not really on board. If this is the case, you will want to learn more about OCD and ERP treatment before moving forward. Otherwise, you'll be giving pushback the whole way through and doing the bare minimum rather than giving it your all. Perhaps you could connect with other kids who have been through treatment by reaching out to local or national support groups for kids with OCD. Check out resources through the International OCD Foundation (www.iocdf.org), which includes recommended documentaries, books, and local community events. You are most likely to get better if you give it your best (rather than your minimum), and some of these things might make you more willing to do so.

Now that we've gone through some of the most common doubts that interfere with treatment, put a checkmark next to any that you've noticed in your own experience.

Doubts That Interfere with Starting Treatment
❒ "My OCD is different."
❒ "Okay . . . so it might work, but what if it doesn't? What if I'm the one person it doesn't work for?"
❒ "What if it makes me worse?"
❒ "Talking about my problems will just make them worse."
❒ "My OCD isn't really a problem" or "It's not that bad."
❒ "I'll just stop one day" or "I'll grow out of it."
❒ "I tried treatment before, and it didn't work."
❒ "I don't know what life is like without OCD."
❒ "I believe my OCD."
❒ "I'm not ready to work on it."

Hopefully, despite some of these doubts, you're willing to accept the challenge and start taking control of OCD. (And if not, we'll talk about other ways to build your motivation in the next chapter.)

Barriers That Try to Get You Off Course

Due to the *tricky, sticky, picky* nature of OCD, as you start to push back against your obsessions and compulsions, you may encounter some barriers that OCD tries to put in your way to derail your efforts and make you give up. After all, OCD doesn't like when you go against whatever it's telling you. This next section goes over some of these barriers in detail so you can be prepared to handle them. These blocks and hurdles will try to trick you into backing down, but you don't have to let them get you off course!

"Something bad will happen if I don't do what my OCD wants."

This is a core fear that drives many symptoms of OCD. Although OCD likes to *trick* you into thinking that something bad will happen if you don't give into your compulsions, there usually isn't any evidence that something bad will actually happen. It's all just a bunch of what-if fears that scare you into doing what OCD tells you. For example, let's say that your OCD tells you that you have to flip the light switch on and off four times when you leave your room or something bad will happen to your family. Or perhaps it tells you that you'll unintentionally upset your friend with your words if you don't mentally rehearse what you are going to say to them. In these cases, you need to do an experiment to test out if your fear will come true and see what actually happens. You can do so by living your life *without* doing the compulsion—for example, by leaving your room without flipping the light switch on and off four times or by talking to your friend without mentally rehearsing it first. Then reflect on what *actually* happened and see what you learned from the experiment. These what-if fears are some of the main ways that OCD continues to have a hold on you. It's time to break free from that hold!

"If there's even a tiny risk or chance that my feared outcome could occur, I can't challenge OCD."

Many of us with a *tricky, sticky, picky* brain are nervous to challenge what OCD tells us because we want to be absolutely sure that our fears won't come true. If we don't have that certainty, we find it really difficult to take the chance. Our *tricky, sticky, picky* brains will say, "There's a real threat that something bad could actually happen," so we tell ourselves that we better not risk it! However, as I mentioned earlier, we are already tolerating a small amount of uncertainty and risk every day, in lots of different ways. We eat at restaurants. We get in cars, buses, or trains several times per week. We ride bicycles. We try new activities. We go to the zoo and assume the cage will protect us from the tigers. All of these things have a small but reasonable degree of risk. Similarly, ERP may involve taking small but reasonable risks to allow you to live a full and productive life.

It's also important to remember that just because something is a *possible* risk (i.e., it could occur), it does not mean that it is a *probable* risk (i.e., it is likely to occur). It's important not to confuse the two.

"I won't be able to handle the anxiety."

Interestingly, the anxiety that we experience before we do something anxiety-provoking (what's called *anticipatory anxiety*) is often much worse than what we actually experience in the moment. We might think, "It's going to be horrible, and there's just no way I can handle it!" However, once we're actually in the situation, we often realize that it isn't as bad as we initially thought it would be. Just because you think something will bother you a lot doesn't mean it actually will. When OCD gets weaker and you gain control, many of these concerns tend to fade away too.

Some kids also feel like they can't handle the bodily sensations associated with being anxious. Doctors call this *anxiety sensitivity*. It's like being afraid of being afraid. Kids with anxiety sensitivity tend to expect the worst whenever they feel an increase in heart rate, nausea, or sweating—and then their reaction to those sensations (e.g., "Oh no! Something must be really wrong!") makes their anxiety worse. Instead, those of us with OCD need to train ourselves to not jump to conclusions if we experience anxiety. Rather, we need to remind ourselves that we can get through it and that the anxiety won't last forever!

"What if I can never reverse what I've done?"

For some people, the act of challenging OCD means putting something into the world that feels like it can never be undone. For example, let's say you "contaminate" your wardrobe by mixing clothing items that are perceived to be "clean" with items that are perceived to be "dirty." In this case, you might worry that it'll be too difficult to keep track of the spread of contamination and that you'll never feel clean again. Or maybe you risk losing your perfect streak of straight A's if you limit how often you check (and recheck) your answers on tests. Or perhaps you're worried that if you don't knock on wood four times, something really bad and irreversible could happen, such as someone you love dying. Though I wouldn't encourage you to do things that have a high probability of resulting in serious harm, remember that taking small, reasonable risks is necessary to live a full life. The types of risks you take when you challenge OCD are similar to those that other people take every day. As you gain confidence against OCD, you'll find that these worries won't feel so scary anymore.

"I'll feel really guilty if something bad happens and it's all my fault."

Let's remember that OCD tends to look for ways to get under your skin. It's going to try to come up with the worst-case scenario and make you think that it's going to happen *and* that you'll be to blame if it's something you might have been able to prevent. It might tell you, "You really won't do this one little ritual, that only takes two seconds, if there's a chance that it would really prevent something bad from happening?" This can get into your head and perhaps even make you feel selfish if you don't do absolutely everything in your power to try to prevent the bad thing from happening. Maybe it tells you to wash your hands one extra time because you don't want to be responsible for spreading contamination in the family kitchen and getting your baby brother sick. Maybe it tells you to check the door lock one more time, as you'd be devastated if it was your fault that a burglar got into the house and stole your family's prized possessions.

Let's reflect on these fears for a moment. If something bad were to happen, would others actually place the blame on you? Are you holding yourself to extremely high standards beyond what you'd hold others to? Is it possible that you may be taking on responsibility to prevent something bad from happening when the pressure shouldn't really be all on you? If that's the case, then the best way to stop this cycle is to push back against what OCD tells you to do.

"What if I treat it like OCD and it turns out it isn't OCD?"

Although you can't always be sure of whether or not a worry is related to OCD, it's sometimes not helpful to draw a line between what is or isn't OCD since it's not always as clear-cut as that. It can also lead you to get caught up in trying to figure out what is or isn't OCD, and this itself can become a compulsion. Instead, it's better to just take a good guess about what to do based on what we know about OCD, without spending too much time analyzing this. (Note: If you are spending time trying to make a determination, try to use a rule of thumb to do so in less than one minute to guard against it becoming a compulsion.) If you're on the fence, here are some clues to suggest that OCD may be at play:

1. **Is the current worry similar to the types of worries you've previously had?**

   Many people with OCD have worries that fall along the same themes (e.g., morality, germs, causing harm). That means if your OCD tends to pick on you with fears of causing harm to others—and your current worry is about that too—there's a good chance that it could be OCD.

2. **Do you feel like you have to do something *immediately* to deal with the worry?**

   OCD often makes you feel like you *need* to do what it wants you to do—right then and there—in order to move on. This sense of urgency is a strong clue that it's OCD.

3. **Is there clear and overwhelming evidence that it is *not* OCD?**

   Clear and overwhelming evidence is super obvious and in your face, without you having to search for it. For example, if OCD tends to pick on you with thoughts that you might get contaminated and become really sick, evidence might be clear signs of illness (e.g., constant vomiting, fainting spells, feverish sweating). However, if you're searching for signs and monitoring yourself for illness without any good reason to do so (e.g., measuring your heart rate to see if it is high, constantly checking to see whether you feel nauseous), it is likely that OCD is involved. Unless you have clear and overwhelming evidence that it is *not* OCD, it makes sense to treat your symptoms like OCD and not engage in whatever your *tricky, sticky, picky* brain wants you to do.

4. **Consider others' or your own past behavior.**

   What would other people do in this situation? Can you look to others as a guide for typical behavior? What about yourself? Was there a time in the past when OCD wasn't present and you faced a similar worry and handled it differently? These are all clues as to whether OCD may be involved.

If you're still unsure after you consider these four clues, the best advice is to treat it like OCD and see what happens!

"I wouldn't be able to deal with it if my fear were to actually come true."

Of course, you don't want your fear to come true, but if it did, I want you to consider the possibility that you could actually handle it. People often have a lot of anticipatory anxiety that they won't be able to get through something, but somehow they do. Has there ever been a time before when you thought you couldn't do something, but in the end, you got through it?

Like I've mentioned before, the experience of having a fear come true may even help you. For example, if you spend years being afraid of vomiting, and then you finally vomit, you may learn, "That was a little gross, but it was only temporary and I got through it." Maybe you are super nervous about making a mistake on a homework assignment, and once you do, you realize that it isn't as big of a deal as you thought it would be. You still get a good grade in the class, and it doesn't make much of an impact at all. It can actually be a good learning experience to deal with situations that you thought you wouldn't be able to handle. Often, you find that you handle them better than you thought you would.

I know that some OCD fears might be even worse, such as your house burning down or a loved one dying, and it certainly would be very upsetting if such things were to happen. If they were to actually happen though, it's likely that there would still be some ways for you to move forward. For example, if your house burned down, you'd probably be really sad that you lost a lot of things that were important to you. You'd probably stay with a relative or friend, or in a shelter or hotel, until you found a new place to live. You'd likely have to borrow some things from others or buy new things. It might be really difficult to deal with, but you'd take things day by day, and it would likely get easier over time. Somehow, you'd find a path forward. So, if you can think through the plan of what would *actually* happen if your fear were to come true, it might help you realize that there would be a way through it. If you're unsure what that plan would be, you can talk to a parent or therapist about it. (Note: Just don't let this become a compulsion to talk through or plan *everything*.)

"I'll go crazy if I go against what my OCD wants."

This is a common worry that a lot of people with OCD have. People worry that if they go against their OCD, their anxiety will increase, and it will continue to go up and up and up . . . until they eventually go crazy. However, as we discussed in chapter 2, your body eventually adjusts to anxiety, and you either see a decrease in it or you get used to it so that it doesn't actually bother you as much anymore.

Now that we've gone through some of the most common barriers that interfere with treatment, put a checkmark next to any barriers that have tried to prevent you from pushing back against OCD.

Barriers That Try to Get You Off Course
❒ "Something bad will happen if I don't do what my OCD wants."
❒ "If there's even a tiny risk or chance that my feared outcome could occur, I can't challenge OCD."
❒ "I won't be able to handle the anxiety."
❒ "What if I can never reverse what I've done?"
❒ "I'll feel really guilty if something bad happens and it's all my fault."
❒ "What if I treat it like OCD and it turns out it isn't OCD?"
❒ "I wouldn't be able to deal with it if my fears were to actually come true."
❒ "I'll go crazy if I go against what my OCD wants."

Are there any other doubts or barriers you've had that weren't mentioned? If so, write them down and then think of what you can say back to them based on what you've learned so far!

Other Doubts or Barriers	What You Can Say Back to OCD

SUMMARY

In this chapter, we've gone through some of the most common doubts and barriers that can show up throughout your journey to challenge OCD. These doubts and barriers tend to have the sole purpose of psyching you out and trying to get you off course, but remember that you have the power to make sure that doesn't happen. In the next chapter, we'll discuss how to get you even more motivated and prepared to stop your *tricky, sticky, picky* brain from running the show. If you take ownership of the process and stay committed, it'll be worth it!

CHAPTER 8

Building the Motivation to Challenge a *Tricky, Sticky, Picky* Brain

If your *tricky, sticky, picky* brain is causing you lots of problems and making you feel worried, scared, or upset, that might be enough to motivate you to put in the work to break the cycle of OCD. However, if you're still not quite sure whether you're ready to take these next steps, then it's important to build some motivation. That's the focus of this chapter. With that in mind, take some time to reflect on the following questions to see how motivated you are to make some changes to help you take control of OCD.

0 1 2 3 4 5 6 7 8 9 10
inch

Importance: On a scale of 1 to 10 (where 0 = "not important at all" and 10 = "extremely important"), how *important* is it that you make these changes now? ______

Readiness: On a scale of 1 to 10 (where 0 = "not ready at all" and 10 = "extremely ready"), how *ready* are you to make these changes now? ______

Confidence: On a scale of 1 to 10 (where 0 = "not confident at all" and 10 = "extremely confident"), how *confident* are you that you can make these changes? ______

If any of your answers were rated lower than a 7, what would it take to move you to a higher number? Would things have to get even worse? Would you have to miss out on more things to finally feel like it's time to fight back against OCD? Would you want more supports in place to feel more confident that you can do it? Write down any ideas you can think of that would help move your numbers up on the scale. Keep those in mind as we talk more about your motivation.

What would make you feel more strongly about the **importance** of making these changes?	
What would make you feel more **ready** to make these changes?	
What would make you feel more **confident** about making these changes?	

What You've Lost to OCD

If you're still on the fence about whether to push back against OCD, it can be helpful to think about how OCD has impacted you—and specifically what you've lost to OCD. Sometimes that allows you to recognize the importance of putting in the work to make a change, even if it feels tough. Here's a list of some of the many ways that OCD can cause problems. Go through this list and check off all of the ways that OCD has interfered with your life.

General

- ❒ Makes everyday tasks and activities more difficult
- ❒ Causes you to feel anxious or stressed a lot of the time
- ❒ Causes you to miss out on living life as fully as you'd like to
- ❒ Makes you dread part of your day (e.g., getting ready for bed) because OCD has made it so tough
- ❒ Causes you to be rigid and inflexible about things having to be done a certain way
- ❒ Leads you to struggle with change
- ❒ Causes you to feel hopeless or wonder, "What's the point?"
- ❒ Makes you question your religion or faith

Health

- ❒ Makes daily personal hygiene tasks (e.g., brushing your teeth, going to the bathroom, showering, or getting dressed) more difficult
- ❒ Prevents you from getting to bed on time because of rituals (e.g., repeating routines, seeking reassurance, excessive praying, making sure that things are "just right")
- ❒ Makes it difficult to fall asleep due to obsessions that keep you up
- ❒ Physically harms you in some way (e.g., leads to dry hands due to excessive handwashing, causes overexertion due to exhausting and time-consuming rituals)
- ❒ Makes it more difficult to take care of your body (e.g., taking your prescribed medicine, eating a well-balanced diet, following doctor's advice)
- ❒ Causes uncomfortable physical symptoms (e.g., headaches, stomachaches, racing heart)
- ❒ Lowers your mood by making you feel sad, stressed, angry, or anxious

Social Life

- ❐ Leads you to avoid certain activities (e.g., sleepovers, parties) or places (e.g., restaurants, malls)
- ❐ Makes friendships difficult (e.g., not talking to friends as much because you're worried about saying the "right" thing)
- ❐ Makes it difficult to meet new friends
- ❐ Interferes with dating (for older kids)

School

- ❐ Causes you to spend extra time on schoolwork (e.g., rereading, rewriting, or checking)
- ❐ Makes it more difficult to focus or pay attention
- ❐ Causes you to be late to or absent from school
- ❐ Makes test-taking difficult

Family

- ❐ Makes your parents or caregivers do things for you that you could otherwise do for yourself
- ❐ Causes interruptions and changes to family plans
- ❐ Causes others to be late or miss out on things
- ❐ Hurts family members due to feelings of anger
- ❐ Makes mealtimes difficult
- ❐ Leads to arguments in the home
- ❐ Causes siblings to be worried or afraid
- ❐ Makes you hesitant to be honest with family members due to concerns about how they'll respond

Fun

- ❐ Makes traveling or vacations difficult
- ❐ Interferes with hobbies and activities (e.g., sports, gymnastics, dance, art, television, movies, reading)
- ❐ Limits how much time you have to enjoy things

How You Feel About Yourself

- ❐ Makes you feel ashamed or embarrassed
- ❐ Makes you doubt if you're a good person
- ❐ Makes you feel like you're not good enough
- ❐ Makes you doubt whether you can be successful in the future (e.g., getting a job, going to college, having a successful career)
- ❐ Makes you doubt whether you can achieve the things that are important to you (e.g., living alone, buying a home, getting married, starting a family)

Does anything else come to mind when you think about how OCD has interfered with your life? If so, make a note of those things below.

1. ______________________________

____

2. ______________________________

____

3. ______________________________

____

4. ______________________________

____

5. ______________________________

____

What You Have to Gain

Even if your OCD has caused you to lose out on a lot in life, you still might be on the fence about making a change. After all, change can be difficult! However, there are a lot of reasons to challenge OCD now. The main reason is that *rituals don't really work.* While rituals might help you feel better *in the moment*, they only make things worse over the long term by keeping you stuck in a never-ending cycle of anxiety. How many times has OCD told you to do a ritual one time, only for it to then tell you that you need to do it *again*? How often has it convinced you that you'll feel better after doing a ritual, only for you to end up feeling much worse? If rituals worked and actually made things better, you likely wouldn't experience so many negative emotions.

Think about all the time and energy you invest in your OCD. Could that time and energy be better spent elsewhere? What if it went toward working hard in school, spending time with friends, getting better at a hobby or sport, or working toward your goals? What if you were finally able to start doing the things that are important to you? Do you think you'd be happier and less stressed? What would you gain? Go through this list and place a checkmark next to all of the things you might be better able to do if you were to break the cycle of OCD.

General

- ❒ Go about your everyday tasks and activities more easily
- ❒ Focus your time and energy on things that matter, like your values and goals in life
- ❒ Engage more in life (e.g., traveling, being more willing to try new things)
- ❒ Have more time for yourself

Health

- ❒ Make daily personal hygiene tasks (e.g., brushing your teeth, going to the bathroom, showering, getting dressed) easier
- ❒ Have an easier time falling asleep; have better sleep habits
- ❒ Take better care of your body (e.g., taking your prescribed medicine, eating a well-balanced diet, following doctor's advice)
- ❒ Feel better physically (e.g., having more energy)
- ❒ Improve your mood

Social Life

- ❒ Participate in more social activities (e.g., sleepovers, parties) and go more places (e.g., restaurants, malls)
- ❒ Improve friendships (e.g., talking to and spending more time with friends, having a more enjoyable time with friends)
- ❒ Have an easier time dating (for older kids)

School

- ❐ Pay better attention in class
- ❐ Manage time spent on schoolwork more efficiently
- ❐ Make test-taking easier
- ❐ Be on time for school; attend more regularly

Family

- ❐ Have a more pleasant home environment (e.g., improvements in communication, nicer conversations)
- ❐ Improve family relationships (e.g., feeling more harmony with parents, getting along better with siblings, spending better quality time)
- ❐ Help your family to manage plans and schedules more easily
- ❐ Help your family feel relief
- ❐ Have an easier time during mealtimes
- ❐ Build more trust with family

Fun

- ❐ Get back into your hobbies and extracurricular activities
- ❐ Travel or vacation more easily
- ❐ Increase the amount of time you have for fun

How You Feel About Yourself

- ❐ Improve your self-esteem
- ❐ Feel more confident that you can do difficult things
- ❐ Feel more hopeful about the future
- ❐ Feel excited about things to come (e.g., getting a job, going to college, having a successful career)
- ❐ Feel more hopeful about achieving the things that are important to you (e.g., living alone, buying a home, getting married, starting a family)

What else might you gain from taking action?

1. ______________________________

____

2. ______________________________

____

3. ______________________________

____

4. ______________________________

____

5. ______________________________

____

What's Your *Why*?

We've gone over many of the ways that OCD makes life difficult (i.e., what you've *lost* to OCD) and considered how your life could be better if OCD wasn't the boss (i.e., what you have to *gain*). With that in mind, it's time to start putting all this information together to identify your *why*. That is, why is it worth it to challenge OCD? To help you get started, I'll first share why I decided to challenge my OCD. Hopefully, you can then think of your own reasons for challenging OCD.

Why I Decided to Challenge My *Tricky, Sticky, Picky* Brain

When I was in ninth grade, I got to a point where I was so frustrated by my OCD. I was mentally and physically exhausted. I was spending hours per day on my rituals to try to get through the day, only to have to go through it all again the next day . . . and the next day . . . and so forth. It seemed like a never-ending hill, and the hill got bigger and bumpier as I went on. Whenever I thought I was nearing the end of a compulsion, my *tricky, sticky, picky* brain would tell me that it still wasn't good enough and that I had to do more. It was never satisfied, and I was sick of it. OCD was also affecting other areas of my life:

- **My health:** I had trouble falling asleep due to obsessive thoughts, and I went to bed late because I was spending time doing needless rituals before bed.
- **My friendships:** I avoided going out with friends because I felt incapable of managing OCD-related anxiety. I didn't want something to trigger my OCD that

might cause me to have an anxiety attack in front of them. I worried that I'd have to call my parents to go home and wouldn't know what to tell my friends.

- **My family:** I asked my parents to do a lot of basic things for me because it was too difficult to do them myself.
- **My schoolwork:** I was often distracted by worry thoughts and urges to do rituals. Homework became super stressful, as OCD thoughts would bombard me whenever I tried to focus.
- **My ability to enjoy life:** I spent hours doing rituals instead of spending that time playing sports or hanging out with friends.

OCD had taken too much from me, and I didn't want it to take any more from me. So, I decided that I'd had enough and I wasn't going to let OCD control me anymore. I wanted to be able to live my life based on what I wanted to do—and not based on OCD's rules. That was my *why*!

Now it's your turn! Although it can be hard work to challenge OCD, think about everything we've talked about in this chapter and ask yourself, "Why is it important for me to do it anyway?" Then write down the top five reasons for you to challenge OCD.

1. ______________________________

   ____

2. ______________________________

   ____

3. ______________________________

   ____

4. ______________________________

   ____

5. ______________________________

   ____

"[My OCD] was causing too many arguments with my parents, especially at bedtime, and causing a ton of stress in our home. I wanted more peace and better relationships at home."

—AMAYA, AGE 11

"I felt stressed all the time. I was either stressed when doing rituals, or worried about what OCD symptom might trigger me next. I felt miserable and constantly on edge, and I didn't want to feel so stressed out all the time."

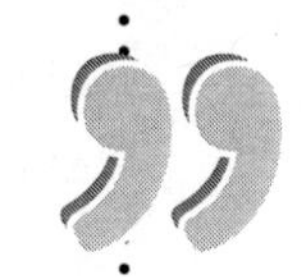

—JOHNNY, AGE 14

Rewarding Your Hard Work

Hopefully, you can see that there is so much to gain by challenging OCD, with the greatest reward being how much better you will feel. However, to increase your enthusiasm even more, it's a great idea to incorporate rewards to help you stay motivated! As you start taking actions to challenge OCD, track your efforts and reward yourself with something special for your hard work. For example, if you face a fear that you have been avoiding, perhaps you plan an outing with a friend as a reward. If you save some time in the evenings because you're able to resist your rituals, maybe you watch your favorite television show. Building in rewards can help you feel extra good about whatever challenges you take on.

To make a reward plan, I recommend choosing a few challenging but manageable goals each week to focus on. You can identify goals by yourself, with your parents, or with a therapist. For example, you might have a goal to resist your nighttime rituals, leave something feeling "uneven" before you exit a room, or let worrisome thoughts be there without counteracting them. There are a lot of different ways that you can create a reward system based on these goals. One way is to give yourself a point for each goal you complete. The more goals you complete, the more points you earn. You can then exchange your point earnings for rewards or privileges. For example, maybe 5 points earns a later bedtime on the weekend while 10 points earns you a visit to your favorite restaurant. Some kids are extra motivated to save their points up for really big or special rewards, so work with your parents to establish a point system that works well for you. Here are some examples of potential rewards:

- Watch your favorite TV show or a movie
- Have your parents make your favorite meal for dinner
- Purchase a small gift for yourself (e.g., new sports equipment, art supplies)
- Get extra screen time or time to play video games
- Go to bed later on the weekend
- Visit the pool or beach
- Get extra reading time at night
- Go on a trip to the park

- Do a special activity (e.g., mini golf, pottery, painting)
- Choose a local event to attend
- Have one-on-one time with a family member
- Go out for ice cream or another dessert
- Choose the game for family game night
- Get your nails done
- Bake cookies
- Take a bubble bath

Another option is to work toward the same goal(s) every day for one week. If you meet your goal(s) a certain percentage of the time by the end of the week, you could get a bigger reward. I like to aim for completing 80 percent of my goals in order to get a bigger reward, as that takes a consistent amount of effort but also doesn't feel too strict. A goal of 80 percent shows that you are determined to challenge OCD, but it also gives you a bit of a buffer if you have some days that are a bit more difficult. The practice and repetition of working on the same goals each day to ensure you're above your 80 percent weekly average is also a great way to get stronger against OCD.

I recommend making a visual chart to track your goals, like the example here, though you can also use another method to track your efforts and successes (e.g., putting pennies or marbles into a jar, placing stickers on a chart). Even adults use rewards to help them follow through with goals, since rewards are motivating regardless of our age. Try to think of rewards that will be exciting and encouraging for you.

Weekly Goal Chart

Goal	Sun	Mon	Tues	Wed	Thurs	Fri	Sat	Number of Times Goal Was Completed
Refrain from reassurance-seeking about food	✓	✓	×	✓	✓	✓	×	5
Limit showers to fifteen minutes	×	✓	✓	✓	✓	✓	✓	6
Do not Google health concerns	✓	✓	✓	✓	✓	×	✓	6
							Total	17

I completed my goal 17 out of 21 times = 81% goal completion

If I complete more than 80% of my weekly goals, then I'll reward myself with a trip to the trampoline park.

Can you think of anything else to help you be successful in reaching your goals? Did you identify rewards that you are excited to earn? Would it be helpful to share your goals with your family or friends? Might it be useful to put reminders and words of encouragement around your room? How can you stick it out and persevere, even if it feels tough? It's important to think about what you can do to help set yourself up for success so you can reach your goals!

Hopefully, this chapter has helped you build the motivation to challenge OCD, as motivation is a key ingredient to successful change. Another important ingredient is *follow-through*, which basically means that you need to make a commitment to stay the course and not give up. One way to stay the course is to be aware of any tricks that OCD might throw your way, which is the focus of the next chapter. By uncovering the ways that OCD tries to have power over you, you will have effective tools to be strong against it.

CHAPTER 9

How to Be *Really* *Good* at This!

Since we've already gone over a lot of the basics to gain control over OCD, it's time to dive into some insider tips to make sure you are *really* good at overpowering it. These tips will help you learn the ins and outs of OCD so you can feel super confident in your ability and stay one step ahead of whatever OCD tries to throw at you.

Tip 1: Know Thy Enemy!

To be extra prepared against OCD, it's helpful to consider the ancient phrase "Know thy enemy," which means that you need to understand your opponent to win against them. If you recognize your enemy's strategies or battle plan before or as it's happening, it gives you a significant advantage over them. For example, in sports, it's important to study the opposing team's strengths and weaknesses to figure out the best strategy to play against them. If you know the plays in the opposing team's playbook, you'll know what to expect and be ready to compete (and hopefully win!).

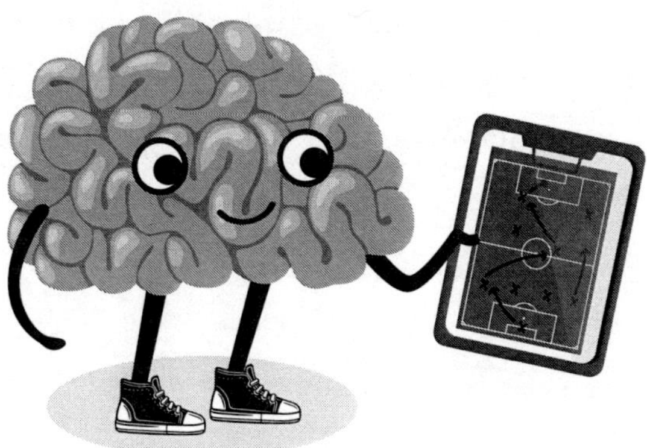

Just as it's helpful to *know thy enemy* in sports, you can become really good at noticing when OCD is trying to trick you. That's because OCD tends to use a lot of the same tricks again and again, with kids all over the world. These tricks can be convincing, but they are usually just lies! If you can learn what they are, you can keep yourself from falling for them. Let's go through several of these tricks together to see if your OCD has used them to try to trick you into doing what it wants. Check off any of the tricks that you've noticed in your own thinking. For the items that you've checked off, write an example of how your OCD has tried this trick on you.

Trick: *"I just need to do one ritual and then everything will be okay."*

Examples:

- "All I need is for Mom to give me reassurance one time, and then I'll feel better."
- "I just have to check once, and it won't bother me anymore. Once is no big deal."
- Your own example: ____

  ____

  ____

Truth: OCD doesn't let people off the hook so easily. It lies. It tells you that if you just do XYZ, you'll feel better, but it is rarely satisfied that easily. In fact, rituals tend to lead to more rituals! For example, if you get reassurance from your mother, OCD will often find something wrong with it. It will tell you that the tone she used wasn't really convincing or that a word she said didn't feel exact enough, which makes you doubt what she said. You feel like the reassurance didn't count, so you ask her to repeat it or say it in a different way, or you might rephrase the question to see if she gives you the same answer. As you do all this, you may even start to get frustrated with her. "Shouldn't my mom know exactly what OCD wants and answer me in precisely the right way?" OCD might then tell you to ask someone else just to be sure. Think about how many times OCD has told you that you "just need to do something one time," only for that not to be true. This trick allows OCD to keep a hold on you by convincing you that relief is just around the corner—and unfortunately, that's a big lie.

Trick: *"This situation is different."*

Examples:

- "It makes sense for me to check in this situation. The threat seems real this time."
- "Those other concerns were clearly based in OCD, but this one isn't."
- Your own example: ____

____

____

Truth: OCD will try to convince you that the situation in front of you is unique or different in some way, so the strategies you've learned to fight OCD don't apply *this time*. Maybe it tells you that there is a "real risk," so you should do what OCD wants. How many times have you thought that a certain symptom was "different," only for this to turn out to be untrue? Sure, it's *possible* that the situation is different, but it's not *probable*. This is just a common trick that OCD uses to scare you into doing compulsions.

Trick: *"This symptom is the worst ever. It's the one that is going to take me down. I may have been able to challenge the others, but not this one."*

Examples:

- "I was able to tolerate being unsure of those other things, but I definitely can't handle being uncertain about this. It would bother me forever and ruin my life."
- "Last time was easy compared to this. There's no way I can manage this."
- Your own example: ____

____

____

Truth: When you're in the throes of OCD, the situation in front of you can seem like the *worst ever*. Your *tricky, sticky, picky* brain will tell you that all previous symptoms weren't actually as serious as this one, so you definitely can't challenge this one. It makes you feel that the risk is too great and that this time the bad outcome is *actually* going to occur. It might also bully you into thinking that you're simply not strong enough to handle it, so you should just give in to OCD. All of this is just OCD's attempt to psych you out.

Trick: *"I'm already at risk, so I can't do anything else."*

Examples:

- "I've already been in contact with too many germs, so any more will definitely make me sick."
- "I've tempted fate too many times already. If I do anything else, something bad will surely happen."
- Your own example: ____

____

____

Truth: OCD likes to look for an "out." It tries to find excuses to persuade you to give in rather than fight back. It also tells you to "play it safe." If you've taken some steps to challenge OCD, such as doing a few exposures, it may tell you that something bad will *surely* happen if you push it any further because you've made yourself more vulnerable. It may tell you that you're tempting fate by doing so many exposures and that something bad is bound to happen if you keep it up. Remember that OCD's goal is to do whatever it can to convince you to give up fighting it, so don't fall for it!

Trick: *"My OCD is under control, so it's no big deal if I give in to just a few things."*

Examples:

- "I can just do this ritual once or twice since it's a new symptom that isn't too strong yet, and then I'll stop."
- "OCD isn't a big problem for me anymore, so it won't matter much if I do one extra check this time."
- Your own example: ____

____

____

Truth: OCD has a way of sneaking back into your life. It will tell you that you are doing fine with managing your OCD, so it won't make a difference if you just do a few compulsions. Unfortunately, if you give in, OCD takes it as a sign that you have some areas of weakness, and it often tries to find more ways to pick on you. It will attempt to add small things little by little until all of a sudden you're overwhelmed and left wondering how OCD got so strong again. The best thing you can do is to be aware of this happening so you can put an end to it as soon as you can.

Trick: *"It's not the 'right' time to work on this."*

Examples:

- "I have a paper due Friday and a test next week. I have too much going on right now to risk feeling anxious."
- "I have a vacation coming up, so I don't want to do any contamination exposures this week in case I were to get sick."
- Your own example: ______________________________

____

____

Truth: It is unlikely that you will ever feel *totally* ready to challenge your *tricky, sticky, picky* brain. OCD wants you to wait until the conditions are perfect and everything feels right, and it will continue to delay and delay things so treatment never has a chance to occur. Perhaps you worry that you have too much on your plate and that a particular challenge will push you over the edge, so you end up procrastinating on it. Although some flexibility is reasonable, since there certainly could be other things going on in your life that make it tough to do exposures at certain times, you don't want to put off challenging OCD forever. Otherwise, it will stay in control. Therefore, it's a good idea to set a reasonable time frame for doing tough exposures so you can stay on track toward accomplishing your goals.

Trick: *"I can't trust my memory."*

Examples:

- "I think I zoned out while reading the instructions, so I should read them one more time to be sure that I didn't miss anything important."
- "I can't remember for sure if I locked the door."
- Your own example: ______________________________

____

____

Truth: Those of us with *tricky, sticky, picky* brains often doubt our memories. We get really bothered if we feel uncertain about something, so we do whatever we can to feel more certain. For example, we might check or repeat things over and over to try to feel sure about something. Unfortunately, this repetition does the opposite of what we want it to do. In fact, it actually makes us distrust our memories even more! That's because a new memory is created each time we check something. If we check something five times, we then have five memories of checking floating around in our heads. If we check ten times, we have ten different memories floating around in our heads. We then start to blur these different memories and don't know which one to trust. Our memories also become a bit distorted when there are several of them competing against each other for space in our heads. All of this tends to confuse things even more.

Since so many people with OCD doubt their memories, researchers have actually studied whether people with OCD have worse memory functioning than those without OCD. Interestingly, they've found no differences in memory functioning between people with and without OCD! The only difference is that people with OCD are *less confident* in their memories, but their actual memory capabilities aren't any worse. So, although you might feel that you can't trust your memory, the lesson here is that you probably can. You just need to develop more confidence that you can. By practicing the strategies in this book, you should be able to develop that confidence!

Trick: *"I need to make sure I'm treating my OCD in the 'right' way. I shouldn't do anything to challenge it because I don't want to mess anything up."*

Examples:

- "I know I'm supposed to change the way I react to my scary thoughts, but I don't know exactly what I'm supposed to do with this *new* thought. I'll just wait until I talk to my therapist again."
- Maybe the strategies I've learned don't apply to this one."
- Your own example: ______________________________

____

____

Truth: If you struggle with perfectionism or "just-right" symptoms, you might feel like you have to be "perfect" when using strategies to combat OCD. Perhaps you feel the need to be completely accurate when describing your symptoms to a parent or therapist because you're worried that any inaccuracies will lead you to get the "wrong" advice. Unfortunately, if you start to analyze everything you are doing to fight back against OCD, it can cause you to become overwhelmed, which may result in you doing nothing at all.

The reality is, there isn't just one way to challenge OCD—there are a lot of different ways! Since there are so many different ways to fight back against OCD, it's helpful to know that you don't have to do things perfectly to gain control over it. Instead of overanalyzing how you will respond to each trigger, try to make a decision about what to do in one minute or less. For example, perhaps OCD is making you anxious about what shirt you are going to wear since it tells you that the two shirts you are considering are both tainted for different reasons. Instead of endlessly overthinking how to proceed, decide on one of these two shirts in less than one minute so that you aren't stuck obsessing about what the "right" or "best" choice is. You could also flip a coin so your choice is truly random. Though it's important to use the treatment strategies in this book, it doesn't mean you have to use them "exactly" or "perfectly" in order to make strides against OCD.

Trick: *"I can't continue on with this exposure. It's too much and I can't handle it."*

Examples:

- "The anxiety is too much for me to bear! I must abort!"
- "This feels tougher that I thought it'd be, so I should stop."
- Your own example: ______________________________

  ____

  ____

Truth: OCD can be relentless in trying to psych you out. If you become super anxious during an exposure, it may tell you that you can't handle it because it wants you to give up midway through the exposure. Unfortunately, if you give up too soon, you won't learn from the experience. Instead, you'll think, "Whew! That was too much. I couldn't handle that, so I can never do it again." However, if you stick it out, you'll learn, "That was tough, and I didn't think I could get through it, but I did. I'm more capable of getting through tough things than I thought." For exposures to have the most pay-off, it's important to see them through. If you have OCD, chances are that you're dealing with anxiety on a daily basis. So, if you're already going to be anxious anyway, it makes sense to be anxious for a brief period of time (i.e., during an exposure) so you can eventually become less anxious overall.

Trick: *"Hmm . . . this super small thing could be a sign of big danger."*

Examples:

- "This chicken tastes a little off. It probably means it's contaminated."
- "That reddish smudge on the hotel carpet could be blood, which means that we'll probably end up in a dangerous situation if we stay in this room."
- Your own example: ____

____

____

Truth: Those of us with OCD tend to hyperfocus (or "zoom in") on signs of potential danger and fixate on things that could go wrong—all while ignoring indicators that everything is probably fine. (This goes back to the thinking traps that you learned about in chapter 4.) For example, if you're concerned about the quality of the lettuce in a salad, you might focus on a small brown mark on one leaf that could indicate that the lettuce is bad. Or if you're worried about getting sick from germs at a restaurant, you might focus on a smudge on a cup and take that as evidence that the dishes weren't washed properly. In short, if we're *searching* to see if something is wrong, we're likely to *find* something that seems wrong. OCD then uses that as evidence to support whatever worries we have. It is important to be aware of this tendency so you can remind yourself to think about things in a more balanced way.

Trick: *"I need to fix or solve something right now."*

Examples:

- "I can't deal with the uncertainty. I won't be able to do anything else until my parent answers my question."
- "I only have a small window of opportunity to deal with this or it will be too late, so I must act now."
- Your own example: ____

____

____

Truth: If something feels urgent and all-consuming—like you have to do it *right now*—it's a strong clue that OCD may be at play. OCD often tries to convince you that the symptom in front of you is the most important thing in the world and that you can't move on to anything else unless you deal with whatever it wants. It will try to trick you into thinking that your entire future will be ruined by this one thing unless you deal with it *right now*. Unfortunately, this is just another scare tactic that OCD likes to use, but if you recognize it—along with the stomach-sinking feeling that often comes with it—it can remind you not to fall for this trick.

Trick: *OCD tries to turn exposures into compulsions.*

Examples:

- "I was less anxious after doing an exposure since I learned that my worry didn't come true. But now OCD wants me to 'check' and 'reassure' myself by immediately doing an exposure each time I have a new OCD thought so I can reassure myself that I won't act on it."
- Your own example: ____

  ____

  ____

Truth: This is a very sneaky trick that OCD likes to use to outsmart you and creep its way back in. When you've made progress by doing exposures (often with things that you've avoided), OCD may take those exposures and see if it can turn them into checking or reassurance-seeking compulsions. This can leave you feeling confused about what to do, as you are probably unsure whether you are helping or hurting OCD. In these instances, a good strategy is to do whatever makes you feel anxious. For example, if you feel the need to do something right away to feel better, then don't do that thing. If you have the urge to pick up a sharp object to reassure yourself that you aren't going to do anything harmful with it, then don't pick it up right then. Instead, allow yourself to feel anxious and unsure.

Are there any other tricks your *tricky, sticky, picky* brain uses that weren't mentioned? If so, write them here, and think of what you can say back to OCD in these moments using what you've learned so far.

Tricks	What You Can Say Back to OCD

Tip 2: Play Offense and Defense!

If you want to keep your OCD under control, one of the best things you can do is play both offense *and* defense. This is just like a game of soccer, where you work hard to kick the ball down the field to get a goal (offense) while also guarding your goal to prevent the other team from scoring (defense).

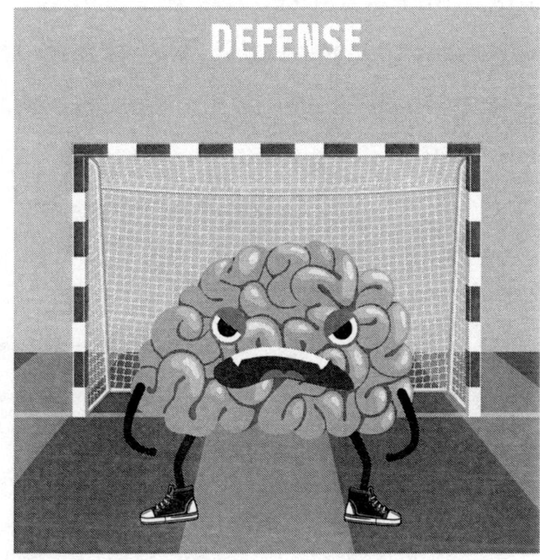

In this metaphor, playing offense means that you go out of your way to score points against OCD. You do this by purposely seeking out opportunities to do exposures instead of waiting for OCD to trigger you. Some kids have the mindset that they don't want to play offense. They think, "Why should I intentionally seek out exposures and rock the boat if everything is fine?" However, there are many reasons for playing offense. Not only does it allow your OCD-fighting muscles to get even stronger, but it puts you at an advantage because when you're the one seeking out the exposures, you often have more control over the situation.

To play defense means that you stay on guard when OCD tries to score points against you *and* you do everything you can to avoid letting it score. When triggers come up naturally as part of your day, you play defense by responding to those triggers with ERP. In addition, if you learn over time that OCD likes to pick on you at certain times (e.g., when you're stressed or tired), you can be prepared and ready to play defense at those times. If OCD happens to score a point against you—meaning that you give in and do a compulsion—you fight back as soon as you realize it so OCD doesn't earn additional points. Remember that you'll be strongest against OCD when you are playing *both* offense and defense!

Tip 3: Stay Strong Through the Tug-of-War

A good analogy when fighting OCD is to think of it like a game of tug-of-war. In tug-of-war, each side keeps pulling and pulling until one side finally can't take it anymore and gives up. You want the side that gives up to be the OCD. See, if you push back against OCD, there's a good chance it'll push back against you. That can be annoying, frustrating, and even discouraging, but if you know you are in a game of tug-of-war, you can be prepared to stick it out. If you stay the course and keep pushing back against it, OCD will eventually back down. Sometimes this will happen quickly, and other times it will take a while. Stick it out for as long as it takes until OCD backs down.

The goal of this chapter was to help you feel even stronger against OCD. By knowing OCD's playbook—and becoming familiar with all of the sneaky tricks that OCD likes to use—you can get really good at recognizing when OCD is trying to manipulate you into doing what it wants. That way you can stay one step ahead and be better prepared to outsmart your OCD!

The next chapter will discuss specific ways your family can help you on your path to gain control over OCD. You can think of your family members as important players on your team in the fight back against OCD. You're the most valuable player on the team, while your family members are teammates there to support your efforts.

CHAPTER 10

How Your Family Can Help You

Family members often play a big role in your life. They often help you learn how to walk, talk, brush your teeth, and prepare for your first day of school. They may help you feel safe, comfortable, and at ease. But since they care about you so much, OCD will sometimes try to take advantage of that by bossing them around. It may bully them into participating in your compulsions, helping you avoid triggers, or changing family routines. OCD can also be really *tricky* in how it gets family members to do what it wants. It might trick them into doing certain tasks for you that would otherwise take you too long, or answering questions over and over again to provide you with reassurance.

If this has happened in your family, you're not alone. In fact, about 90 percent of kids with OCD have family accommodation of some kind. *Family accommodation* is a fancy term that describes how family members are often involved in OCD in some way. It describes all the things your family does to help you deal with OCD in the moment so you can function and get through your day easier.

Here are some of the ways that OCD likes to trick your family members into doing what it wants. See whether you recognize any of these based on your own experience with OCD. Check off any actions that you've noticed in your own home life. For the items that you've checked off, write an example of what happens in your family.

Answering your questions, giving you reassurance, or listening to you confess things

Examples:

- ❒ Reassuring you that your what-if thoughts aren't going to happen
- ❒ Telling you that you're "okay" whenever you have physical sensations that make you worry something is wrong with your health (e.g., pain in your leg, a funny feeling in your chest)

- ❒ Reassuring you that the lights are off or the doors are locked
- ❒ Listening to you confess your thoughts so they can assure you that your thoughts don't make you a bad person
- ❒ Giving you detailed information about where they are going and what they are doing whenever they're going to be away from you
- ❒ Your own example: ____

____

____

Providing items for rituals

Examples:

- ❒ Buying more soap for you because your excessive washing causes you to go through it so quickly
- ❒ Obtaining items around the house for you because you have time-consuming rituals whenever you move between rooms or up and down the stairs
- ❒ Purchasing new items for you (e.g., clothing, groceries, toothbrushes) due to worries that prior items are contaminated
- ❒ Your own example: ____

____

____

Helping you avoid things that trigger your OCD

Examples:

- ❒ Ordering for you at restaurants because you worry about saying the wrong thing
- ❒ Taking a different route while driving so you don't pass by certain triggers
- ❒ Avoiding crowded places (e.g., restaurants, malls)
- ❒ Your own example: ____

____

____

Directly participating in your compulsions

Examples:

- ❒ Inspecting your food to confirm that it is safe for you to eat
- ❒ Driving you back to a previous location so you can check something or complete a ritual
- ❒ Participating in a specific nighttime routine so it's done "just right"
- ❒ Making decisions for you because OCD causes you to doubt your decisions
- ❒ Your own example: ____

____

____

Modifying the family routine

Examples:

- ❒ Delaying dinner plans until you are done completing rituals
- ❒ Being late to work because your time-consuming rituals delayed the day
- ❒ Lying next to you until you fall asleep at night or staying with you all night
- ❒ Changing who does certain household chores because those chores trigger your OCD
- ❒ Your own example: ____

____

____

Doing things for you that would otherwise be your responsibility

Examples:

- ❒ Checking over your homework to make sure it was completed correctly
- ❒ Wiping you after you use the bathroom (so you don't end up wiping excessively or washing your hands excessively)
- ❒ Preparing food for you because it would be too time-consuming for you to do yourself

- ❒ Handling "contaminated" objects for you so you don't have to deal with them
- ❒ Your own example: ____________________

____

____

Are there any other ways your family members are involved in your OCD? Write them down here.

1. ____________________

____

2. ____________________

____

3. ____________________

____

4. ____________________

____

5. ____________________

____

Unfortunately, the more your family accommodates your OCD, the more difficult it is for you to do things on your own—and the stronger your OCD gets. Here is a diagram showing how the cycle of family accommodation keeps OCD strong:

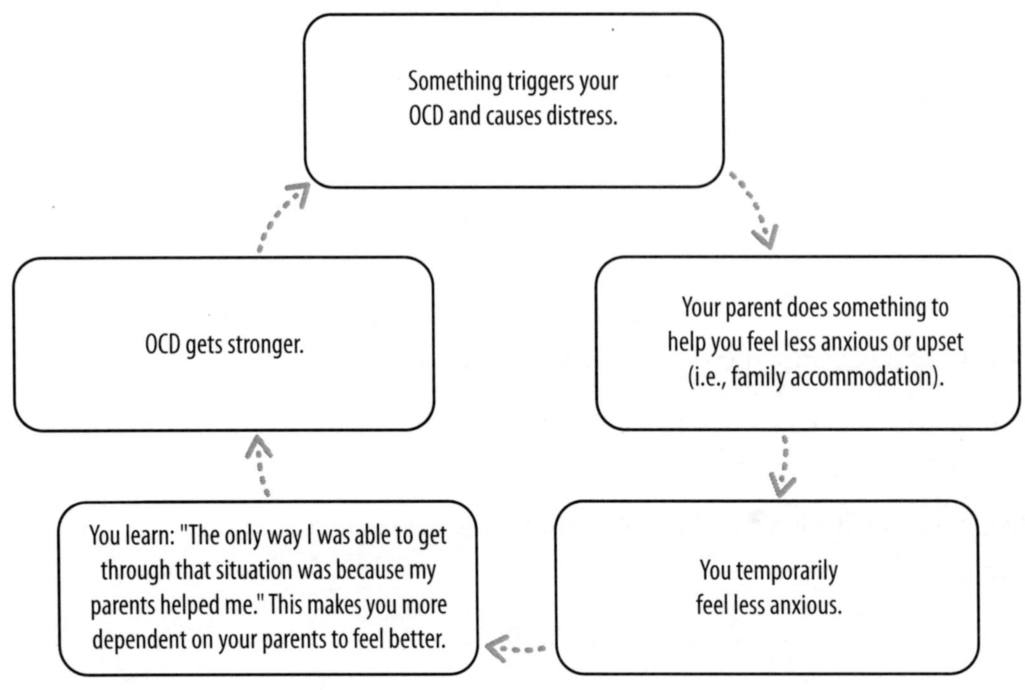

If you identified ways that your family members are participating in your OCD, the only way to break the cycle is to gradually lessen what they do. Though this can feel scary at first (it was a bit nerve-racking for me!), it will ultimately help you feel stronger and better about managing OCD on your own. The following table has some examples of how you can take small steps to decrease family involvement in OCD.

OCD Symptom	How to Challenge OCD
Asking your parents repetitive questions throughout the day to get reassurance	• Set a limit on the number of questions your parents will answer each day, and gradually reduce this number each week. • Refrain from getting questions answered regarding certain topics (e.g., health, school). Start with topics that are easier to challenge and work your way up to more difficult topics. • Limit yourself to one question-and-answer session with your parents per day—and put a time limit on it. Maybe you start with a limit of fifteen minutes and gradually reduce the number of minutes.
Having your parents check over your food because you're worried about contamination	• Don't have your parents inspect your food before you eat it. Start with foods that are "easier" and work your way up to not having them check foods that feel "more difficult." • Don't have your parents answer questions about your food (e.g., "Is it expired?"; "Do you think it looks funny?"; "Is it cooked fully?"; "Does it smell bad?"). You can do this for easier items first and then work up to foods that feel more difficult. • Don't have your parents confirm that they washed their hands prior to preparing your food.

Work Together!

Any changes to family accommodation are best achieved by having a mutually agreed upon plan for how your family members will reduce their involvement in your rituals. It's best to work together as part of the same team. Then you all need to follow through in doing your respective parts! That means your *family* shouldn't surprise you by making changes that you aren't expecting, and *you* also need to follow the plan by not trying to convince your family members to give up on the plan. Understand that when your parents stop giving into your rituals, it's because they care about you getting better, and they want to help you be strong against OCD. Your OCD may even try to trick you into saying to your parents, "Don't you love me?" or "You must not care about me!" In these moments, and all those moments that you feel weak, it can be even more important for them to be firm. Remember that OCD is difficult on your parents too. It is upsetting for them to see you having a difficult time, so it's important for them to stay strong with whatever plan you have established and not give in to your OCD.

Practice Being Flexible

Even if you establish a well-thought-out plan to reduce your family's involvement in your OCD, there may be times when it doesn't go exactly as hoped. Remember that OCD is *picky*, and it often wants things done a certain way. There is no such thing as a perfect parent, and your parents also can't read your mind. Given that, it's important not to abandon the plan just because something doesn't go as expected. For example, maybe a parent gives you reassurance with a slightly different phrase or tone of voice than you were expecting, so it doesn't feel "exactly right." Perhaps they mess up one step of the bedtime routine, so you feel like you need to do it all over again.

If things don't go exactly as planned, it is good practice for you to be flexible and to try to "go with the flow." Chances are you already have practice doing this in other areas of your life! For example, have you ever been to a restaurant only to learn that they were out of your favorite meal? Or have you ever made a plan with friends only to have to change plans because of sickness, the weather, or something else that came up? As with these examples, you sometimes need to accept that things are often out of your control. That way, you can aim to still follow through with the exposure, even if unexpected changes occur.

Help Your Family Help You

In addition to reducing how much your family is involved in your OCD, it can be helpful to brainstorm other things that they can do to better support you. Here's a list of some ideas:

- Tell your family how they can encourage you. Are there certain supportive phrases or comments that would be helpful? Any that you find annoying or that you wouldn't want them to use? (Note: They shouldn't encourage you by accommodating your symptoms.) Your parents may not completely understand all the details of your OCD, but they can still show you love, care, and concern.

- Consider ways your parents can participate in your treatment. Maybe you come up with exposure ideas that you can do together. That will help them see what you are going through and will also teach them how to better support you.
- Have a plan for what your parents will do if they see you ritualizing. Should they try to stop you, or is it better to leave you alone? When parents see you in distress, they may have the protective urge to interrupt you in the middle of a ritual, but that often makes the situation worse since you may feel like you need to start the ritual over. Instead, have a plan for what everyone will do in these situations. (Note: An exception to this is that it is appropriate for parents to intervene if there are concerns about your safety or the safety of others.)
- Work with your parents to break difficult challenges or exposures into smaller, more manageable steps.
- Have a way to communicate about OCD in public (e.g., code word or nonverbal signal) in case you are having a tough time and could use support but want to be discrete about it.
- Celebrate victories and small improvements. Work with your parents to come up with a reward system to track your goals and reward your efforts (see chapter 8).
- Spend time with your parents talking about and doing *non*-OCD things. Don't let OCD take complete control of your relationship with each other.
- Talk about your OCD with your parents. Try not to get discouraged if they don't respond well at first or if they seem worried about what you told them. They aren't experts, and some parents need a bit more time to better understand what their child is going through. Often, an experienced OCD therapist can be a big help with this. If it's uncomfortable for you to talk to your parents about your OCD, maybe you limit it to weekly fifteen-minute check-ins and avoid talking about your OCD at other times.

If you have siblings, consider how much or how little to share with them about your OCD. This may depend on a variety of factors, such as their age, what they might understand, your relationship, what your parents want, and whether they might have their own challenges.

Just remember that OCD affects your siblings too. They might feel on edge about what they can say or do around you since they don't want to do anything that might cause you anxiety. They might feel sad or guilty if they accidentally trigger your OCD and it ends up causing a lot of stress in the home. They might want to help, but you aren't in a place where you want their help. They might start to keep more to themselves because they don't want to add any additional burden to the family.

Or maybe they don't understand the gravity of what you are dealing with, and they assume you're doing it just for attention. Perhaps there are even times when they purposely trigger your OCD to get under your skin. If any of these things are occurring, it's important to figure out with your family how to handle it. Maybe you all talk about things together or your parents talk to your siblings separately.

Just as it's important for your parents to learn about OCD, it's also helpful for your siblings to know what is going on, as once they are educated about OCD, they'll be in a much better position to support you. If they are old enough, share resources with them so they can better understand what OCD is really like and help them empathize with what you are going through. If you have a therapist, you can even have a family session to explain things further and give your sibling a chance to ask questions. There should also be boundaries in place so that OCD doesn't control your siblings either. Hopefully, your parents can also make it clear that there will be consequences if your siblings tease you about your OCD or purposely trigger you.

This chapter reviewed the many ways that OCD can impact family members. It also described how you can take small steps to lessen their involvement while working together to gain control of OCD. Part of this process involves accepting that your parents are going to have to set limits when it comes to your rituals. It's understandable if you get upset or angry when this happens, because it can definitely be difficult. However, the reality is that they are setting limits because they care—not because they want to see you upset. In the next chapter, we'll discuss how you can handle any setbacks on your journey to challenging OCD and provide you with some tips to avoid falling back into old habits.

CHAPTER 11

Maintaining Improvements and Getting Even Better

When you have OCD, chances are that your *tricky, sticky, picky* brain will try to fall back into its old ways. While your OCD could certainly go away completely, slipups and setbacks are extremely common. New types of symptoms or "flavors" of OCD might even pop up, as OCD likes to try to jump to new things. It may show its face again months, years, or even decades later, so it's important to have a plan if and when this happens. The good news is that once you have gotten a handle on the skills to combat OCD, you will have these skills forever!

You'll also see that the same strategies you use for one OCD symptom will also work for other symptoms, even if the concerns are completely different from whatever bothered you before. So, don't be hard on yourself if setbacks occur because you can always get OCD back under control. Setbacks do not have to be anything more than bumps in the road, as long as you act quickly and apply what you know to keep OCD from worsening.

In fact, each setback that you work through strengthens your *muscle memory*, which is the ability to do something (often a specific muscle movement) more accurately and effectively after you do it repeatedly. Examples include riding a bike, playing the piano, or typing on a computer. Once you've learned these skills, you don't have to start from scratch each time you go back and do them again, even if it's been a while, since muscle memory brings the skill back to you more quickly. Similarly, the more you consistently practice your OCD-fighting skills, the more you'll improve them!

Taking a proactive approach to handling setbacks is what doctors call *relapse prevention*. To practice relapse prevention, you'll need to get really good at recognizing warning signs that OCD is trying to take back control. This will allow you to prevent smaller setbacks from turning into bigger OCD episodes. You'll also need to think about the times when OCD is more likely to pick on you so that you can be extra prepared for when OCD tries to take over. Let's go over the actions that make up a relapse prevention plan—keeping OCD at bay and *you* in control.

> **Relapse prevention:** Strategies to help you maintain your progress and minimize the chance of OCD symptoms returning after you've challenged them

Brainstorm Potential Triggers

Certain situations may make it more likely that OCD will try to pick on you. This can include big changes to your routine (e.g., moving, traveling, holidays) or high-pressure situations (e.g., exams, school performances, family events). You may also be more likely to give in to OCD if you haven't slept well or are sick. OCD likes to sneak-attack during these times if it thinks that you are more vulnerable. If you are able to identify these situations ahead of time, you can be extra prepared so OCD is less likely to win. Write down some of the situations that may be triggers for you.

1. ______________________________

   ____

2. ______________________________

   ____

3. ______________________________

   ____

4. ______________________________

   ____

5. ______________________________

   ____

Incorporate Exposures into Everyday Life

Remember from chapter 9 that you shouldn't *just* play defense and wait for OCD to pick on you. You also need to play offense and purposely find opportunities to do exposures as often as you can. By practicing every day, you keep your skills sharp. It also helps you be much more confident in your skills and much less likely to forget them. This is just like someone who puts in the work to build stronger muscles. If they stop lifting weights, their muscles will weaken. But if they keep lifting weights, their muscles will get stronger. Don't let your skills weaken.

Engage in Approach Behavior, Not Avoidance Behavior

Doing exposures can feel scary and cause a lot of what-if thoughts in your mind, like "What if I touch the doorknob and get sick?" or "What if I don't say my nighttime prayers four times and something bad happens to my family?" However, remember that just because you have what-if thoughts doesn't mean that they are likely to come true. Unless there's clear, overwhelming evidence that you're in danger, you want to keep doing exposures that challenge your OCD. A "chance" of something bad happening is *not* evidence. Instead, "clear" and "overwhelming" means that the evidence is so obvious that you don't have to look for it. It's as if the evidence is staring you right in the face—for example, the evidence that you're in danger because a lion is three feet away from you and roaring in your face.

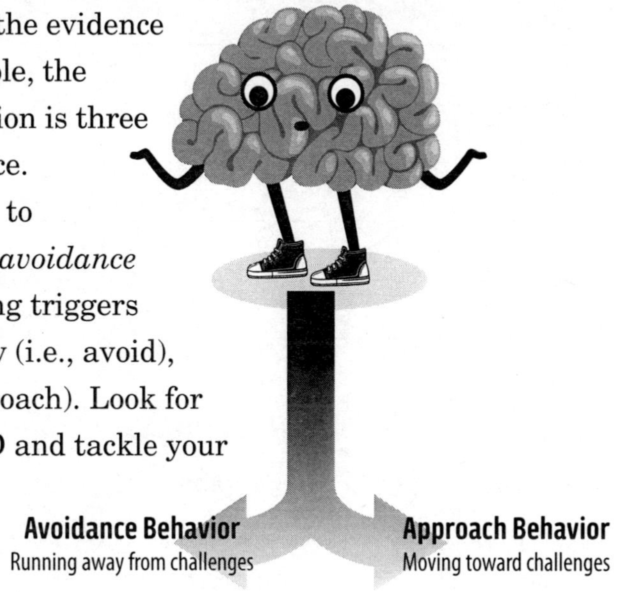

In the absence of true danger, it's best to engage in *approach* behavior rather than *avoidance* behavior. This means that when something triggers your fears or makes you want to run away (i.e., avoid), you should try to face it instead (i.e., approach). Look for opportunities to get stronger against OCD and tackle your fears head-on when you are confronted with new challenges.

Avoidance Behavior
Running away from challenges

Approach Behavior
Moving toward challenges

Identify Warning Signs ("Red Flags") of OCD

How do you know if OCD is starting to act up again? How might you know if it's trying to come back but with a new symptom? Here are some early warning signs that OCD is trying to rear its head:

- You feel like you have to do things a certain way.
- You're more bothered by minor things.
- Tasks are starting to take longer.
- You feel like you have to fix things or address them right away.
- You're starting to avoid things that you didn't avoid before.
- You're depending on others for things that you used to do yourself.
- You have worries that are consistent with a previous "theme" of your OCD—for example, being concerned about doing the "right" or moral thing or worrying about causing others harm.

If you recognize any of these red flags, it may be a sign that OCD is trying to sneak its way back into your life and that you should intervene as soon as possible. Write down some of the signals that are warning signs for you.

1. ____

____

2. ____

____

3. ____

____

4. ____

____

5. ____

____

Tackle OCD Symptoms Sooner Rather Than Later

It's important to fight back against OCD as soon as you notice it picking on you because if a symptom is newer, it is less *sticky*, meaning that it's easier to challenge. You know how glue is more flexible before it hardens? It's the same thing with OCD in that symptoms are easier to challenge if you tackle them before they've gotten the chance to become so rigid. For example, if you're taking a shower and all of the sudden you get the urge to wash your body in a particular order, you can tell yourself, "I didn't wash in any particular order yesterday or any days before that, so this is probably just OCD trying to pick on me."

The problem is that some kids give in to their OCD in these moments since it doesn't seem like a big deal to do it "just this once." They tell themselves, "I'll wash my body in this specific order just this one time." However, this then leads to them giving in again and again, and they're suddenly feeling stuck in a washing routine that they've been doing for months. Instead, knock out new or returning symptoms as soon as you catch them. In my experience, kids rarely complain that they wish they waited longer to fight back against their OCD—it's always that they wish they fought back sooner.

Practice Self-Care

It might sound simple, but taking care of your mental and physical health—for example, by getting enough sleep, drinking water, eating healthy, spending time doing things you enjoy, and exercising—can go a long way in protecting you against OCD. This is known as practicing *self-care*. Think about the types of self-care you can do to keep your mind and body feeling strong. For example, does it energize you to have some quiet time? Does it improve your mood to spend time with family or friends? All of these things help protect against OCD. Write down some ways you can practice self-care.

1. ______________________________

____

2. ______________________________

____

3. ______________________________

____

4. ______________________________

____

5. ______________________________

____

Identify Supports to Help You Deal with Setbacks

It's important to decide what role your parents and family members will have in helping you deal with setbacks. For example, if you notice that you are falling back into old habits, will you tell your parents or family members? Should your family point out to you any new or worsening symptoms they notice? Would you be okay if they brought it up to you? If so, can you have a plan for how they'll approach it with you in a way that feels supportive and from a place of love and concern instead of feeling punitive or negative?

If your symptoms worsen, you also want to identify at what point you should seek professional help. Depending on whether you previously worked with a therapist, how will you decide if it's necessary to schedule a booster session? For example, do you want to first try to come up with exposure exercises on your own? Or do you want to reach out to a therapist right away? While it is *always* okay to seek help, some kids avoid reaching out to a therapist or put it off. They may minimize their setbacks and deny that their OCD is getting worse.

Therefore, you'll want to think about the behaviors that indicate it is time to seek help. Maybe you seek help if OCD is taking up more than one hour per day. Or maybe you seek help if you are struggling to complete important tasks, like getting your homework done. These signs will vary from person to person, but it's important to think about what they would be for you so you can keep an eye out for them.

Practice Self-Compassion

Self-compassion is about treating yourself with kindness and gentleness when setbacks occur. Although it can feel discouraging when you slip up and give in to your OCD, it doesn't mean that you are weak or a failure, or that something is wrong with you—it is simply common for setbacks to occur. While it is important to be consistent in using the skills in this book, you do not have to be perfect in using them to keep OCD under control. Have compassion for yourself if mistakes occur. You aren't all-knowing and you don't have to be perfect. If you give in to your OCD and your symptoms worsen, just try to learn from it and do better next time instead of beating yourself up over it.

Self-compassion statements can be helpful for when you have a setback. Some examples are "This setback doesn't define me" and "I can learn from this and do better next time." If you're having a difficult time coming up with self-compassion phrases, think of what you might tell a good friend going through a similar tough time. Write down some possible self-compassion statements that might be helpful for you.

Me

1. ____

____

2. ____

____

3. ____

____

4. ____

____

5. ____

____

SUMMARY

The goal of this chapter was to help you establish a plan to keep OCD under control. Although it's easy to feel discouraged if you notice OCD worsening, it is important to approach relapse prevention with the mindset that you can handle anything OCD tries to throw at you. Remember that each setback and hurdle you work through will strengthen your muscle memory for fighting against OCD. By identifying potential triggers that make you vulnerable to OCD, you'll be on guard and ready in case OCD tries to show up. All of this practice will help you feel even more confident that you've got this! In the next chapter, I'll introduce you to some incredible friends I've met—all with OCD—and talk about how they used the skills in this book to take back control from OCD.

CHAPTER 12

Friends with a *Tricky, Sticky, Picky* Brain

I mentioned in chapter 1 that tons of kids struggle with a *tricky, sticky, picky* brain. Since many kids with OCD don't know others who are going through the same challenges, I thought it would be helpful for me to introduce you to some of the friends with OCD that I've met. By learning about other kids with OCD—some with very different symptoms—it can help you realize how many of us have a *tricky, sticky, picky* brain. Getting to know other people just like you can help you feel a lot less alone. I know it helped me a lot!

So, let's meet some of my awesome friends with OCD! After you learn about each friend and the problems their OCD causes, we'll talk about some of the tools they used to gain control over OCD—specifically, cognitive restructuring and ERP exercises that helped them push back against OCD.

DOUBTING DANNY

Are you mad at me?

Danny constantly doubts whether he may have accidentally done something that could cause harm in some way. Even though other kids really like him, he worries about whether he might have done something to cause his friends to be upset with him, so he replays past conversations in his head to try to remember what he said and how his friends responded, all to figure out if they're mad at him. If he's still unsure, he'll ask his friends, but most of the time they don't even recall what Danny is talking about.

Danny also doubts whether he left the door unlocked or his hair dryer plugged in, so he'll check such things several times before he can move on. Whenever he uses something that involves a plug or electricity before he leaves the house, he takes pictures of the appliance after he has unplugged it so he can refer to them later to make sure it's off; he thinks that he'd never forgive himself if something bad happened and it was his fault. Danny also gets anxious when he is around cleaning products in the kitchen, as he'll doubt whether he may have accidentally poured a chemical into his younger sister's drinking cup instead of milk or juice, so he'll end up smelling the drink to check it or pouring it out altogether to redo it.

In addition, Danny doubts whether he put his homework in his bookbag, so he'll often check two to three times in the morning to feel sure (even after putting it in there the night before). He doesn't want his teacher to think he's a bad student who doesn't care about grades. When he turns in exams, he tries to get a mental image of the completed test questions so that he feels sure that he completed the test fully. Danny is sick of dealing with the mental exhaustion that comes with doing all of these rituals, and he is frustrated that he feels like he can't trust his memory.

Here is how Doubting Danny got his *tricky, sticky, picky* brain under control:

- **Cognitive restructuring:** Danny identified a variety of anxious thoughts and thinking traps, such as "I need to be sure that I didn't say anything offensive to my friends" (*intolerance of uncertainty*), "My teacher will think I'm a bad student if I forget my homework" (*mind-reading*), and "I have to be sure that things are unplugged so nothing bad happens" (*intolerance of uncertainty, inflated responsibility*). However, Danny realized that nothing bad happened during previous years when he didn't do these rituals, which he used as justification that he could probably trust himself more than he thought. He then established more balanced thoughts, such as "It's normal not to have 100 percent certainty, and I can cope with some degree of doubt," "Even if I make a mistake in a conversation, a longtime friend will probably be understanding," and "Most of the time, when I'm uncertain about something, it doesn't lead to a disaster." Given these new more balanced thoughts, Danny felt more willing to take the risk to challenge his OCD through ERP.
- **ERP:** Danny engaged in exposures in which he practiced reducing all of the rituals he was doing to feel sure about things. Instead of going back to check things or take pictures, he made a goal to move forward even if he got a thought that he forgot something or did something harmful. Initially, Danny worried that "this would be the time" that something bad would actually happen, but he pushed on despite these thoughts, and eventually the thoughts started to occur less and less.

DOUBTING DANNY'S ERP CHALLENGES

- Limit checking of the hair dryer and door to two times before leaving the house.
- Allow thoughts that friends could be mad at him to be present in his mind, but don't ask friends for reassurance.
- Check only once in the morning to make sure his homework is in his bookbag.
- Do not check in the morning to make sure his homework is in his bookbag (and instead accept that he already checked the night before).
- Leave the house without taking pictures of electrical appliances.
- Do not check the hairdryer to make sure it is off after using it. Then take a thirty-minute walk around the block.
- Turn in exams without taking a mental image of the completed test.
- Pour a drink in a cup and drink it without smelling it (while a cleaning product is somewhere in the kitchen but not on the kitchen counter).
- Pour a drink in a cup and drink it without smelling it (while a cleaning product is nearby on the kitchen counter).
- Serve drinks to family members without any checking or smelling rituals (while a cleaning product is nearby on the kitchen counter).

Here is what Danny learned: Over time, Danny found that he could trust himself a lot more than he thought, and he became a lot more confident in himself. He also found that nothing bad happened when he eliminated his excessive checking behaviors, which helped him see that they weren't necessary. This was anxiety-provoking at first, but he was able to go about daily activities much more easily as time went on.

MORAL MARCUS

Marcus feels like he always has to do the "right" thing, and he feels guilty if he thinks he has done anything wrong. He'll worry about whether he was truthful in conversations and wonder, "What if I lied?" He'll then go over past conversations in his head, mentally reviewing them to reassure himself that he was truthful. If he doubts whether he was completely honest during a conversation, he'll awkwardly follow up with the person and find a way to reexplain what he meant, as he doesn't want to have lied.

Marcus also gets unwanted, bothersome thoughts that he thinks are immoral and inappropriate. He'll think of curse words and worry that he'll suddenly blurt them out in school or at his place of worship, so he has been avoiding religious services. He feels like he must confess to his parents whenever he has these thoughts so they'll reassure him that he is a good kid. If he has a negative thought about someone, like "My teacher is a jerk," he'll also say something nice to that person as a means to cancel out the negative thought.

Marcus also confesses to his parents whenever he thinks he may have done something bad, such as if he didn't help someone when he could have, or if he snuck a snack that he wasn't supposed to eat. He also gets really upset and down on himself about past actions that he thinks were more serious, like the time he tricked his brother into doing something that broke the house rules, so he'll go over such things repeatedly with his parents to make sure they completely understand exactly what happened and can reassure him that it wasn't a big deal.

If Marcus feels like he has been wasteful in some way, such as letting the water run while brushing his teeth or throwing out food because he didn't like it, he tells his parents, asking them to reassure him that it is okay. If Marcus passes by trash or litter on the ground, he feels like he should put it in a trash can or he'll feel guilty that he isn't doing everything he can to help the environment. Marcus feels incredibly overwhelmed with trying to be a good kid who always does the right thing.

Here is how Moral Marcus got his *tricky, sticky, picky* brain under control:

- **Cognitive restructuring:** Marcus identified anxious thoughts and thinking traps, such as "I should always do the right thing" (*should statements, perfectionism*), "I must know for sure if I said something inaccurate or I lied" (*intolerance of uncertainty*), "I must confess if I think I have done something bad" (*inflated responsibility*), and "I might blurt out curse words that come into my mind" (*thought-action fusion*). Marcus realized that he was living by unrealistically high standards that left him feeling like he was not good enough, so he created more balanced thoughts, such as "I can be honest and strive to do what's right without holding myself to standards of moral perfection," "Having an intrusive thought doesn't make me a bad person," and "I'm still a good person, even if I make mistakes." Marcus then used these new thoughts to help motivate him to challenge OCD with ERP exercises.
- **ERP:** Marcus began to do exposures in which he left things feeling uncertain—like whether or not he said something inaccurate, or if others think he's a good kid—and he allowed the presence of bothersome thoughts and questions without trying to push them away.

MORAL MARCUS'S ERP CHALLENGES

- Do not review past conversations (and instead allow himself to feel uncertain if he was truthful).
- For things he has already confessed to parents, do not tell them again for at least twenty-four hours.
- Do not reexplain to someone what he meant in a previous conversation.
- Attend a religious service and stay even if he has intrusive thoughts of curse words.
- Do not receive reassurance that he's a good kid if he confesses something to his parents.
- Do not confess to his parents if he catches himself being wasteful.
- Do not confess to his parents if he has intrusive thoughts of curse words.
- Do not confess minor things to his parents (like not helping someone when he could have or sneaking a snack).
- Do not cancel out negative thoughts with positive thoughts.
- Receive a limit of five instances of reassurance per day.

Note: Before working on ERP for these concerns, it is important to have clear exceptions about what things you should always report to parents—for example, if there is clear and overwhelming evidence of danger that would warrant a hospital or police visit, or if someone's safety has been actually threatened. Otherwise, OCD will try to tell you that everything needs to be shared. Remember, the *possibility* of danger does not equate to evidence of actual danger!

Here is what Marcus learned: Marcus learned that he was capable of tolerating uncertainty and that he didn't need to be sure about *everything* in order to feel better. Once he stopped engaging with his thoughts by doing compulsions, he was able to distinguish OCD thoughts from his personal values and recognize that "inappropriate" thoughts are not necessarily a reflection of his true morals.

SOMATIC SCARLETT

Scarlett gets very anxious if she has any sort of physical symptom that feels unusual to her. She worries that a headache might mean that she has a brain tumor, or that any pain, even if it is minor, could mean something serious. She finds herself checking her pulse throughout the day to make sure her heart rate is normal. Scarlett often examines her body for signs of illness, researches her symptoms on the internet, and tells her parents anytime she feels the least bit "off," just in case something bad happens and they need to know what might be wrong in order to help her. She also asks her parents to reassure her that she is okay, and sometimes she wants them to take her to the doctor to be sure.

Scarlett also finds herself constantly thinking about what's going on in her body, like how often she swallows and if she is breathing enough. She often gets stuck thinking about whether she needs to swallow. She pauses throughout the day to monitor her breathing and confirm that she is taking full, deep breaths. When Scarlett finds herself focused on these things, she then worries that she won't be able to stop thinking about them. These worries take a lot of mental energy and often distract Scarlett from doing schoolwork, spending time with friends and family, and falling asleep at night.

Scarlett is also terrified of getting cancer, so she doesn't want her parents to use anything with chemicals inside the house, like insect repellant or cleaning supplies. On her request, her family only uses natural products instead. She repeatedly checks product labels to be sure that they are "safe." All of this is extremely stressful for Scarlett and her family, as she wants to live her life without worrying so much.

Here is how Somatic Scarlett got her *tricky, sticky, picky* brain under control:

- **Cognitive restructuring:** Scarlett identified several unhelpful thinking patterns, such as "I assume the worst when I notice a physical symptom" (*catastrophizing*), "If I have a brain tumor and don't get surgery immediately, it could cause permanent damage. Then, I won't be able to learn anymore, go to college, or get a job one day" (*snowballing*), "I might choke if I don't pay close attention to my swallowing while I'm eating" (*overestimating threat*), and "I can't move on unless a doctor reassures me that I'm healthy" (*intolerance of uncertainty*). Scarlett considered the evidence and realized that she was focusing a lot on unlikely what-if thoughts rather than facts. She established more helpful thoughts, such as "It's normal for people to experience aches and pains that come and go, so there's no reason to assume a headache is a brain tumor," "The somatic symptoms I notice have never turned out to reflect a serious problem with my body," and "My body is capable of managing its functions without me having to monitor every sensation." After establishing a more balanced outlook, she was motivated to take the risk and challenge her fears by engaging in ERP.

- **ERP:** Scarlett started doing ERP exercises in which she stopped checking and researching her physical symptoms. She refrained from engaging with health-related worries unless there was clear and overwhelming evidence of illness (e.g., her symptoms continued to worsen or noticeably interfered with her ability to function). She also allowed herself to notice whenever she swallowed and breathed without trying to monitor or analyze these bodily functions. Further, she gave permission to family members to use whatever cleaners and substances they wanted to use in the home, and she stopped avoiding these things.

SOMATIC SCARLETT'S ERP CHALLENGES

- Wait five minutes to check her pulse when she has the urge to check it.
- Limit checking of her pulse to three times per day.
- Wait one hour to tell her parents about a lower-stress health symptom.
- Do not check any product labels when at a friend's house.
- Do not check her pulse for one full day.
- Do not check to make sure she is taking full, deep breaths.
- Delay researching health symptoms on the internet for twenty-four hours after she notices a symptom.
- Her parents use one preferred chemical cleaner in the home (rather than all natural products).
- Exterminator sprays inside the house and she doesn't get reassurance about what chemicals are used.

Here is what Scarlett learned: Scarlett learned to stop hyperfocusing on any physical sensations she experienced, rather than misinterpreting normal bodily sensations as signs of serious illness. She accepted a reasonable degree of uncertainty about these feelings and made more balanced decisions about what did and did not warrant medical attention. Through these exercises, Scarlett learned to live a more fulfilling life without being limited by her fear of developing a serious health issue.

"JUST-RIGHT" JUAN

Juan feels really uncomfortable if things aren't "just right." He has a tough time explaining what exactly bothers him, but he'll sometimes get a feeling that things are "off" or "wrong" in some way. He feels like he needs to repeat certain behaviors, such as closing drawers or doors, until it feels "just right." He constantly touches and taps things because he feels that he needs to in order to feel okay. If Juan touches something with his left hand, he feels that he has to touch the same thing with his right hand to make it even, or he otherwise gets a feeling of things being unbalanced. If Juan thinks he said something that doesn't sound "right," like mispronouncing a word or believing he said a sentence not smoothly enough, he'll say it again or repeat it under his breath so he ends up saying it "right."

Juan also wants the conditions to be "just right" before he can fall asleep at night, as he doesn't want anything to jeopardize his ability to fall asleep. As a result, he checks to make sure his blinds are fully closed, his closet door is shut, and the temperature is at a specific number. He sometimes checks these things several times. He also wants to be sure that he has an empty bladder before he goes to sleep. Sometimes he'll get out of bed two or three times to try to pee again, just to make sure he has emptied it fully. He also wants to pee at the last possible second before he gets in the car with his family to go anywhere, even if it is a short drive, because he doesn't want to risk feeling uncomfortable and possibly peeing in his pants. All of this causes him to get to bed much later than planned, and it can also be disruptive to his family's plans.

Here is how "Just-Right" Juan got his *tricky, sticky, picky* brain under control:

- **Cognitive restructuring:** Juan recognized that he was experiencing several anxious thoughts and thinking traps, such as "I can't tolerate the sensation of feeling 'off'" (*"I can't handle it"*), "I need to say things 'just right'" (*perfectionism*), "I won't sleep if I don't feel completely relaxed" (*catastrophizing*), and "If I don't pee before I get in the car, I'll pee in my pants" (*overestimating threat, fortune-telling*). Juan considered the evidence and realized that there wasn't a practical need for him to make things "just right." Juan then established more balanced ways of thinking, such as "I can tolerate feeling uncomfortable," "I'll manage even if I have trouble falling asleep," and "I haven't peed in my pants since I was a toddler, but if it does happen, I'll figure out a way to clean myself up and move on." Juan then used these new, balanced ways of thinking to encourage himself to challenge OCD with ERP exercises.

- **ERP:** Since Juan's *tricky, sticky, picky* brain was trying to boss him into doing things until he felt "balanced" or "right," his goal was to purposely do things that left him feeling "unbalanced" or "wrong." By engaging in exposures that triggered an internal state of things being not "just right," he practiced leaning into feelings of discomfort rather than trying to make sure he felt comfortable.

"JUST-RIGHT" JUAN'S ERP CHALLENGES

- Leave a drawer open a little bit.
- Put the temperature on a different ("wrong") number at bedtime.
- Purposely leave doors around the house feeling "wrong" before he leaves for school.
- Touch things with his left hand only (and do not follow up with his right hand to make things even).
- Do not repeat words or sentences that he feels didn't sound "right."
- Go to the bathroom fifteen minutes before getting in the car for a one-hour drive.
- Intentionally leave the closet door and blinds open at bedtime.
- Use the bathroom once right before getting into bed. Do not check his bladder again for at least thirty minutes.

Here is what Juan learned: As Juan repetitively did things that left him feeling "unbalanced" or "wrong," he realized that it started to bother him less and less. His thoughts went from "I can't handle feeling not 'just right'" to "I can handle feeling a little weird." Though he initially felt physically uncomfortable during these exposures, he later found that he moved on from them more and more quickly as time went on, and they stopped bothering him altogether. Once he stopped touching and tapping things repetitively and refrained from making excessive trips to the bathroom before riding in a car or going to sleep at night, he also found that he was able to go about his day with much greater ease.

MAGICAL THINKING MILA

Mila worries that if she thinks about something, it makes it more likely to happen. She also worries that if she has a "bad" thought, it means she must want it to happen. When she has such thoughts, she knocks on wood because she believes that it will either prevent those things from occurring or prove that she doesn't really mean the "bad" thoughts. Mila also has a bedtime ritual of saying a certain apologetic phrase at bedtime ("I didn't mean any 'bad' thoughts that I had today") as extra protection against bad things happening, just in case she missed knocking on wood for anything throughout the day.

Mila has certain numbers that she feels are "safe," so she uses them and avoids "unsafe" numbers. She also has a pile of clothes that she avoids wearing because she associates each item with something bad that happened when she wore them previously (e.g., getting in an argument with a friend or getting sick), and she is worried that something bad will happen if she wears them again. Mila often feels on edge because she isn't sure when the next thought will enter her mind and tell her what to do. All of this is causing her a lot of worry and sadness.

Here is how Magical Thinking Mila got her *tricky, sticky, picky* brain under control:

- **Cognitive restructuring:** Mila identified several anxious thoughts and thinking traps, such as "Something bad will happen if I rewear the same clothes" (*repetitive thinking*), "My thoughts reflect what I really want deep down" (*overimportance of thoughts*), and "If I think about doing something bad, I might do it unless I stop myself from thinking it" (*thought-action fusion, need to control thoughts*). However, she realized that there wasn't evidence to support these beliefs. She also realized that she didn't have these compulsions when she was younger, and nothing horrible happened then. She therefore created more rational thoughts, such as "There's no logical connection between my thoughts and the outcomes that I'm afraid of" and "Just because I have an unwanted thought doesn't mean it will come true." These new thoughts helped her feel more willing to engage in ERP exercises.
- **ERP:** Mila engaged in exposures to test out whether her fears came true. She allowed the presence of "bad" thoughts and eliminated the rituals that she was doing in response to them. She also repeatedly sought out exposures with "unsafe" numbers and clothing items that she had been avoiding so she could do experiments to investigate whether those things were actually linked with bad things happening.

MAGICAL THINKING MILA'S ERP CHALLENGES

- Intentionally think about making silly or fun things happen to see if they come true (e.g., her pet dog talking like a human, her favorite singer showing up at her house).
- Take an "unsafe" number of bites of food during a meal.
- Purposely think about minor frustrations to see if she can make them happen to those she loves (e.g., her dad stubs his toe, a bird poops on her parents' car window) without "knocking on wood."
- Wear "tainted" clothing to a neutral event.
- Wear "tainted" clothing to a meaningful event.
- Do not "knock on wood" when she has a scary thought.
- Go to bed without saying her bedtime phrase.

Here is what Mila learned: By doing behavioral experiments such as using "unsafe" numbers, wearing "tainted" clothing, and allowing "bad" thoughts to be present, Mila gained evidence that she could do such things without something catastrophic occurring. This was really beneficial in helping her learn that she didn't need to be scared of her thoughts since they didn't cause things to happen. As a result, Mila was able to start making decisions based on what she wanted rather than letting fear control her.

PERFECTIONISTIC PETE

Pete believes that he has to do things the absolute best way, all the time. If his schoolwork is not completely perfect, he worries that his teachers will think badly of him and that he'll get a bad grade. He erases and rewrites his letters if he doesn't think they are neat enough. He views anything below an "A" as unacceptable, as he worries that it'll interfere with his chance to get into the best possible college. Whenever he has an upcoming test, he starts studying well in advance and will even skip hanging out with friends because he doesn't want to do poorly and end up regretting that he could have done more. He stays up extra late to study, which interferes with his sleep. It also takes Pete a while to get started on assignments and projects because he checks instructions multiple times to make sure he is doing it correctly.

Pete is also particularly fixated on wanting his skin to look as good as possible, so he is very strict with his twice-daily skincare routine to help minimize the chance of any skin-related issues. Unfortunately, this takes a lot of time that he could otherwise spend on other activities. He'll even avoid sleepovers with friends because he doesn't want to miss out on his skincare routine and because he's concerned that they'll judge him if they see what this routine involves. Pete avoids eating certain foods as well because he is concerned that they'll lead to breakouts, and he often begs his parents to take him to the dermatologist so he can be sure that he is doing everything possible to care for his skin.

Pete's perfectionism also interferes with his social life, as he worries about speaking perfectly with friends. He reads text messages over and over before he sends them to make sure he hasn't written something offensive or odd that will make his friends mad or cause them to think he is weird. Sometimes he'll avoid texting his friends at all because it is so difficult for him.

Pete also plays basketball, and he has a rule for himself that he must practice every day to improve his skills. He also feels the need to end every practice session with a successful basket, or he worries that he'll play poorly in his next game. This sometimes causes him to be late to other things. Pete is constantly exhausted because of all the time and effort that goes into trying to do everything perfectly.

Here is how Perfectionistic Pete got his *tricky, sticky, picky* brain under control:

- **Cognitive restructuring:** Pete identified anxious thoughts and thinking traps, such as "If I'm not perfect, I'm a failure" (*all-or-nothing thinking*), "My teachers, parents, and coaches will be disappointed in me if I don't perform perfectly" (*mind-reading*), "I need to do my skincare routine exactly right" (*perfectionism*), and "If I don't end basketball practice with a basket, I'll play poorly in the next game" (*magical thinking*). Pete collected evidence for and against these beliefs, and once he realized that there wasn't much evidence to support his OCD worries, he created more balanced thoughts, like "I can still be really smart and successful in college, even if I am not perfect," "My teachers, parents, and coaches will probably be understanding if I don't perform perfectly since I have a track record of consistently working hard and doing well," "My worth isn't determined by whether or not I have perfect skin," and "It doesn't matter if I end basketball practice with a basket, as I can still play well in the game. Consistency is more important than perfection." Pete then used these new thoughts as motivation to take the risk and challenge OCD by doing exposures.
- **ERP:** Pete started to do exposures in which he risked things not being perfect. He also did exposures in which he intentionally left things imperfect, without fixing them, to see what would happen.

PERFECTIONISTIC PETE'S ERP CHALLENGES

- Write essays without any erasing or rewriting. Allow handwriting to be less neat than it could be.
- Skip one step of his skin care routine.
- Complete a homework assignment using his nondominant hand (whichever hand he doesn't typically write with).
- Ask a teacher for an estimate of how long to study for an exam, and limit his studying to that amount of time.
- Skip his entire morning skincare routine (and instead use the time he saves to attend before-school office hours for extra help).
- Check instructions on assignments only once.
- Purposely end basketball practice on a "miss" instead of a basket.
- Skip two days of practicing basketball at home.
- Send text messages to his friends without fixing misspellings or other mistakes.
- Have a sleepover at a friend's house and skip his entire nighttime skincare routine while there.

Here is what Pete learned: Pete realized that it really wasn't necessary to achieve perfection because the things he feared would happen actually did not happen! He realized that he could still have high standards while striving for things to be "pretty good" or "good enough" rather than perfect. His friends didn't seem to treat him very differently, even if he made mistakes. He even ended on a "miss" at basketball practice and then happened to have one of his best games the next day, which provided some evidence to challenge his belief that it would affect his game. By showing more flexibility and less perfectionism, he was able to devote more time to the things that were important to him, such as spending time with friends and getting a good night's sleep.

EXISTENTIAL EMILIA

Emilia describes herself as a "thinker." She constantly asks big questions about life and the world. She finds herself getting stuck on questions like "What's the meaning of life?" "What's my purpose?" and "Who am I?" She feels like she needs to figure this all out to guide her decisions on what classes to take or clubs to join, as she doesn't want to spend time doing things that aren't in line with her life purpose. Emilia also gets preoccupied with thoughts about what is "real." She finds these thoughts to be overwhelming, confusing, and somewhat scary. Emilia also thinks about how big the universe is and how small she is in comparison, but these thoughts make her anxious, so she tries to distract herself when she has them and push them out of her head.

Emilia also finds herself thinking about death and dying, like what happens when we die or whether there is a higher power. These thoughts make her feel anxious because she can't have certainty about such things. Emilia spends a lot of time researching these questions online and having conversations with friends and family to hear others' perspectives. She often finds herself zoned out in class because she can't stop thinking about it all. She tries to avoid situations, conversations, and places that trigger thoughts about any of these things. Emilia worries that she'll always be stuck wondering about these big life questions.

Here is how Existential Emilia got her *tricky, sticky, picky* brain under control:

- **Cognitive restructuring:** Emilia identified a lot of distressing thoughts and thinking traps, such as "I need to know the meaning of life or else I'll never be happy or fulfilled" (*catastrophizing*), "If I don't know my purpose, then it's pointless to take hard classes" (*all-or-nothing thinking*), and "I have to figure out what happens when we die" (*intolerance of uncertainty*). However, Emilia realized that overthinking wasn't giving her the answers. Instead, it was just keeping her stuck in a cycle of anxiety. She realized that she had already experienced a lot of joy and fulfillment in her life without knowing answers to all of these existential questions, and this evidence helped her create healthier, more balanced thoughts, such as "I am able to live a meaningful life without fully resolving these big life questions" and "I can create meaning in my own life through family and friends, new experiences, goals, and values, rather than identifying one single, clear purpose." These new thoughts helped Emilia become motivated to challenge her OCD through ERP.
- **ERP:** Emilia engaged in exercises in which she stopped trying to answer these big questions. Specifically, she allowed these questions to be present in her mind without trying to solve them or push them out of her head, and she'd instead strive to continue with activities that were a better use of her time

(e.g., homework, extracurricular activities, time with family and friends). She also stopped researching her questions and seeking reassurance from others about their perspectives.

EXISTENTIAL EMILIA'S ERP CHALLENGES

- Write down words that trigger existential OCD thoughts.
- Write statements that reflect uncertainty about existential topics, such as "I am really small in comparison to the universe" and "I might be living in a simulation."
- Read about outer space (e.g., articles from NASA).
- Watch a movie or TV show about outer space, like *E.T. the Extra-Terrestrial*, *Apollo 13*, *Spaceballs*, *The Jetsons*, *The Martian*, or *Star Trek*.
- Do activities that invite sensations of not feeling "real" (e.g., looking at optical illusions or spirals, reading *Magic Eye* books, breathing rapidly to induce feelings of brain fog or detachment).
- Read obituaries of people who have passed away.
- Watch a movie or TV show that relates to the topic of things not being "real" or living in a simulation, like *The Truman Show*, *Wreck-It Ralph*, *Inception*, or *Rick and Morty*.
- Research and write about the vastness of outer space.
- Put glow-in-the-dark stars on her bedroom ceiling.
- Visit a planetarium.
- Watch a movie or TV show with a plot that focuses on death and dying, such as *Ghost*, *Coco*, *Field of Dreams*, *Beetlejuice*, or *The Good Place*.
- Go to a cemetery to visit graves of loved ones who have passed away.

Here is what Emilia learned: Emilia learned to focus on doing things that she felt added positively to her life in the present rather than spend her time trying to answer unanswerable questions. By accepting the presence of uncertainty and staying engaged in day-to-day activities, she was able to cope with these thoughts much better. She learned to simply notice the existential thoughts when they came up without feeling a need to act on them, and over time, the thoughts seemed to have less and less of a hold on her.

CONTAMINATION-CONCERNED CHARLIE

Charlie worries a lot about contamination, to the point that he struggles to do anything without thinking about whether he could get sick from germs or cause others to get sick. As a result of his fears, he tries not to touch things in public (e.g., doorknobs, handrails, classroom supplies) to avoid contact with germs. If he does touch things that he thinks could be contaminated, he is sure to wash or sanitize his hands immediately, as he fears that the germs could otherwise absorb into his skin quickly, and then it would be too late to stop himself from getting sick. This has unfortunately caused him to have dry, cracked, and irritated skin. He also wipes down certain items, and he constantly cleans his shoes and his phone, as he feels that those items are particularly contaminated.

Further, when Charlie takes a shower, he scrubs each body part for two minutes in a specific order to make sure he washes everything thoroughly and feels that he has cleaned sufficiently to be safe from germs. If he thinks he zoned out while washing, he'll wash again to be sure he didn't miss anything, so sometimes his showers take over an hour and cause a lot of stress with getting to bed on time.

Charlie also worries that he could accidentally spread germs when he uses the bathroom or that he won't wipe himself fully. He'll wipe over and over to be sure that he is clean, sometimes to the point that it will irritate his bottom. He'll then excessively wash his hands after using the bathroom since he worries about spreading germs from his hands to other things. He thinks that bathroom germs have a particularly high risk of causing a serious illness. Charlie doesn't think he could ever forgive himself if he was responsible for spreading germs that cause someone else to get really sick or die.

Charlie also gets stressed out in new situations because he tends to immediately focus on all the things that he thinks could be contaminated rather than being present in the moment. He even avoids talking to new people because he is so concerned that he could catch germs from them. Charlie just wants to live his life more normally, without stressing out about germs so much.

Here is how Contamination-Concerned Charlie got his *tricky, sticky, picky* brain under control:

- **Cognitive restructuring:** Charlie identified anxious thoughts and thinking traps, such as "If I touch something contaminated, I need to wash the germs off right away so that I don't get sick" (*overestimating threat*), "I should always keep germs away from those I love" (*should statements*, *inflated responsibility*), and "I can't tolerate it unless I know that I am clean" (*"I can't handle it"*). When Charlie collected evidence for and against these beliefs, he realized that his concerns were exaggerated and unlikely. He then created more balanced thoughts, like "I can take reasonable precautions with germs and still enjoy life without engaging in excessive protections," "It's normal to be exposed to germs, and it doesn't always lead to illness. My body has defenses that are designed to handle exposure to germs," and "It's not all on me to protect others from germs. I can use appropriate safeguards, but I'm not solely responsible for everyone's health." These new, balanced thoughts gave him the confidence to start engaging in ERP.

- **ERP:** Charlie engaged in gradual exposures that allowed him to accept reasonable risks with things he perceived to be contaminated while simultaneously reducing related washing and cleaning compulsions. Specifically, he made goals to reduce his excessive washing and showering routines (e.g., spending less time on each body part, not rewashing himself even if he thought he zoned out, reducing his wiping), and he took gradual steps to achieve them.

CONTAMINATION-CONCERNED CHARLIE'S ERP CHALLENGES

- Wash one part of his body out of order during his showers.
- Touch the family's TV remote without washing or sanitizing his hands first.
- Do not sanitize his hands prior to opening the refrigerator.
- Wash his hands for a maximum of thirty seconds after going #1.
- Do not wipe down his phone before bringing it inside the home.
- Decrease the number of wipes by two (if he normally wipes ten times after going #2, he'll wipe eight times instead) and tolerate the feeling that he might still be contaminated.
- Touch doorknobs at school without washing after.
- Limit himself to wiping five times (after going #2).
- Stop wiping after the first piece of toilet paper without poop stains on it (after going #2).
- Skip one part of his body during his showers.
- Wash his hands for a maximum of one minute after going #2.
- Unless his hands are at least 50 percent covered in *observable* dirt, do not sanitize before touching items in house.
- Wash his body in the shower until he feels 75 percent clean and then don't wash further.

Here is what Charlie learned: As Charlie engaged in contamination exposures, he learned that he could tolerate a reasonable degree of risk from germs, and over time, it became less worrisome to him. He realized that nothing significant or unmanageable occurred when he reduced rituals to help him feel clean. Charlie learned that he could have a much more enjoyable life if he could shift from having perfectionistic standards of cleanliness to having a more practical, balanced approach.

SCARY-THOUGHT SUSIE

Susie gets thoughts and images in her head of scary things happening. She imagines things like someone in her family getting hurt in a bad car accident or an intruder coming into her home and hurting her family. The images can be vivid and realistic, and they are pretty distressing to her. She also gets scary thoughts of doing bad things, such as stealing items in a store, suddenly turning the steering wheel while her parents are driving, or knocking the lunch tray out of a peer's hands when they walk by her in the cafeteria. To feel less worried, she'll do things that make her feel safe, such as crossing her arms when peers walk by her at lunch, putting her hands in her pockets when she is in a store, and sitting in the backseat of the family car so she isn't close enough to reach the steering wheel.

Susie also gets scary thoughts when she is using scissors, like worries that she might lose control and stab someone. Even though these thoughts don't make any sense, she'll hold scissors far away from herself to feel safer, just in case they could come true. What's more is that Susie even gets intrusive thoughts about hurting her baby brother or her pet dog by squeezing them too hard or accidentally doing something harmful without thinking. These thoughts upset Susie a lot, as she doesn't want anything bad to happen to anyone, but the thoughts and images keep popping into her head.

It's important to Susie that she is a kind, loving person, but now she wonders if she is really an evil person who might snap one day and act on her scary thoughts. Susie tries to monitor how she feels when she has these thoughts because she wants to reassure herself that they bother her, but sometimes this just creates more doubt for her. When these thoughts or images pop into her head, she now repeats a phrase in her mind ("I want everyone I love to be safe") because it makes her feel better. Susie is scared to talk to her parents about these thoughts because she worries that they'll be disappointed or that she'll get in trouble.

Here is how Scary-Thought Susie got her *tricky, sticky, picky* brain under control:

- **Cognitive restructuring:** Susie identified unhelpful thoughts and thinking traps, such as "These thoughts must reflect the true nature of what I actually want to happen" (*overimportance of thoughts*), "I must get these thoughts out of my head so I don't act on them" (*need to control thoughts*), "I feel dangerous, so I must be dangerous" (*emotional reasoning*), and "What if I hurt someone and end up going to jail, never see my family again, and my life is completely ruined?" (*snowballing*). Upon checking the facts, Susie recognized a lack of evidence to support her scary thoughts, so she established more balanced thoughts, such as "It's common to experience scary thoughts sometimes, and they don't reflect my actual intentions or desires," "Having intrusive thoughts doesn't define my character," and "I can think something without ever acting on it, and I can recognize these thoughts as just part of OCD." These new thoughts helped her feel more confident about engaging in ERP.
- **ERP:** Susie practiced allowing her scary thoughts to be present without doing anything to push them away or counteract them. She also started to do the things that she was avoiding (e.g., using scissors, going into stores, interacting with her baby brother and pet dog) without taking precautions to keep herself and others safe.

SCARY-THOUGHT SUSIE'S ERP CHALLENGES

- Do not cross her arms when peers walk by with lunch trays.
- Walk through aisles of favorite store with her hands outside of her pockets, pick an item up, and let thoughts of "stealing" be present without trying to push them away.
- Do a family art project at the kitchen table using scissors, making sure to keep them nearby on the table.
- Write a story about her fears of scary things happening coming true.
- Sit in the front seat of the family car while her parent is driving.
- Play with her baby brother or dog while her parent is in a different part of the house.
- Do not do her ritual of saying, "I want everyone I love to be safe."

Here is what Susie learned: Susie learned that she doesn't need to place so much emphasis on her thoughts as being significant or meaningful. Through decreasing safety behaviors, she learned that they were unnecessary, as she didn't end up acting on any of her fears. This allowed her to realize that she could have thoughts about doing scary things without actually doing them. This helped Susie separate her identity from that of OCD.

RELIGIOUS RYDER

Ryder's faith is very important to him, but he is anxious about observing his religion correctly so he does not upset God. If he does not say his morning prayers exactly right, he thinks that they don't count and that something bad will happen to him as a punishment for not taking his prayers seriously enough. This fear often leads Ryder to repeat his prayers over and over until he feels that they are done accurately, which sometimes causes him to miss the school bus in the morning. He also obsesses about whether things he sees might be signs from God, and he'll try to analyze those signs in response. He worries that if he misses a sign, it could have the consequence of majorly impacting his life in some way.

Ryder believes he must show complete devotion to his religion in order to go to heaven, so he'll apologize to God and do additional prayers if he thinks his devotion is in question. If Ryder hears about a different religion, he'll do extra prayers for his own religion to demonstrate how faithful he is. If he has a thought about the devil, he thinks he must have some "evil" inside him, so he prays for forgiveness.

Ryder is adamant about following religious teachings exactly right, but his strictness seems well beyond the observance of others who follow the same religion, such as his peers at his religious school and his parents. For example, Ryder's religion has some rules about foods that he isn't supposed to eat, so he spends a lot of extra time (more than his friends or family) checking food labels to make sure he doesn't eat something that violates the guidelines. Ryder also spends excess time doing a nightly ritual of asking for forgiveness for sins "just in case" he did something wrong that day and doesn't remember sinning.

Here is how Religious Ryder got his *tricky, sticky, picky* brain under control:

- **Cognitive restructuring:** Ryder identified anxious thoughts and thinking traps, such as "Prayers are either done right or wrong" (*all-or-nothing thinking*), "If I don't say my prayers perfectly, they won't count" (*perfectionism*), "If I miss a sign from God, it'll completely change my life for the negative" (*catastrophizing*), and "I should show complete devotion to God" (*should statements*, *all-or-nothing thinking*). He then established more balanced thoughts such as "God doesn't expect perfection. The intention behind my prayer is more important than perfection in how I pray" and "I'm going to have faith and trust that God knows what's in my heart." Ryder's motivation to have a healthier relationship with his religion and God helped encourage him to challenge OCD with ERP.

- **ERP:** Ryder started engaging in daily prayers and religious observance without repeating himself if he made a mistake. He considered what others in his religion did and used that as a guide for his own religious observance, which helped him stop doing extra rituals that were in service of proving his devotion to God. He also stopped analyzing whether things might be "signs" from God since he never reached a definite answer anyway; instead, he just leaned on his faith in God rather than trying to figure out if God was sending him signs that could be easily missed.

RELIGIOUS RYDER'S ERP CHALLENGES

- Read or talk about other religions without doing extra prayers to demonstrate faithfulness to his own religion.
- Do not check food labels in the house (and instead trust that food bought by his parents is in line with food guidelines of their religion).
- Say his daily prayers one time, even if he doesn't feel they are exactly right.
- Read stories of people who believe that their life changed after getting a "sign from God."
- Attend a religious service of another religion without doing extra prayers to demonstrate faithfulness to his religion.
- Refrain from his nightly ritual of atoning "just in case" he sinned.

Note: If OCD focuses on religious observance, it is sometimes helpful to consult with a faith leader in your community to develop exposures that fight back against OCD but do not go against your faith. It's best if the faith leader is knowledgeable about OCD, or if they can collaborate with a therapist so everyone works together as part of the same team, as many faith leaders are not well-versed in OCD. However, it's important that it doesn't become a ritual to talk to a faith leader, as this can easily turn into a reassurance-seeking ritual if you feel like you have to go over everything you do with them.

Here is what Ryder learned: Ryder realized that a lot of the things he felt he had to do in the service of his religion or God were actually things he was doing in the service of OCD. Once he stopped doing such things, he was able to develop a healthier connection to his religion and God. Ryder also realized that he believes in a good God—not a punishing God that would demand perfection. He also reflected on his beliefs and realized that faith is having the courage to live with uncertainty and trusting that God knows what is in his heart. By reducing compulsions, Ryder ultimately learned to have more appreciation for his religion instead of having his religious practice driven by fear.

EMETOPHOBIC ESTHER

Esther is terrified of vomiting, which is a fear called *emetophobia*. She remembers a time in third grade when a friend got sick at school, and she started to fear that the same thing could happen to her. She has been scared of vomiting since then, and she finds herself bothered by thoughts and images related to vomiting, which she wishes would stop. If someone talks about vomiting or she sees something about it on TV, she immediately leaves the situation, as she worries that it could cause her to get sick. Esther doesn't think she could handle it if she vomited, as she worries that she would feel gross, disgusted, and out of control. She also worries that it would be embarrassing if it occurred at school.

In an effort to prevent herself from getting sick and vomiting, Esther inspects her food at home and at restaurants to make sure it is okay to eat. For example, she examines her meat to be sure that it is fully cooked. She'll also seek reassurance from her parents and ask them to check or even taste her food to confirm it is safe to eat. Esther is on edge whenever she eats, and she'll often comment that something "doesn't taste right," which will cause her to stop eating it. She sticks to a limited number of "safe" foods when she isn't with her parents, and the variety of foods she eats has dwindled to fewer and fewer items over time. She sometimes misses meals altogether because she is too nervous and can't bring herself to eat.

Esther worries that overeating could also cause her to vomit as well, so she is sensitive to feeling full and will stop eating before she gets that feeling. She avoids any dairy products before school, just in case something could be spoiled that causes her to get sick at school. She also avoids sitting on one side of the couch at home since she knows her brother vomited there previously. Esther's symptoms are causing a lot of stress, and she has also been missing class due to frequent visits to the school nurse, where she complains that her stomach feels funny and asks if her parents can pick her up. Esther wishes that she could just eat normally without worrying so much about her food and the chance that she could get sick.

Here is how Emetophobic Esther got her *tricky, sticky, picky* brain under control:

- **Cognitive restructuring:** Esther recognized several anxious thoughts and thinking traps, such as "If I have thoughts or images of vomiting, it'll make me throw up" (*thought-action fusion, overimportance of thoughts*), "If I sit on the part of the couch where my brother vomited, I'll get sick too" (*repetitive thinking*), "I'll get sick if I feel too full" (*overestimating threat*), and "It'd be too embarrassing and I'd feel out of control if I vomited" (*catastrophizing, "I can't handle it"*). She then established more balanced thoughts, such as "Stomach discomfort and nausea don't always lead to vomiting" and "Vomiting is unpleasant, but I can handle it if it happens." These new thoughts helped Esther develop willingness to take the risk to engage in ERP.

- **ERP:** Esther started to face things that she had been avoiding, such as watching content that reminds her of vomiting, eating foods that weren't on her "safe" food list, and visiting places that she associated with vomiting. This allowed her to test out her fears to see what would happen. She also imagined the details of her worst-case fear coming true—vomiting at school and feeling embarrassed—to help her work through those emotions.

EMETOPHOBIC ESTHER'S ERP CHALLENGES

- Brainstorm and write slang terms related to vomiting (e.g., *barf, gag, throw up*).
- Sit on the side of the couch that she avoids.
- Listen to vomit sounds (e.g., someone throwing up or making gagging noises).
- Take three more bites past her initial feeling of fullness.
- Eat one food that isn't on her "safe" food list.
- Eat or drink a dairy product before school.
- Write a story about her worst-case fear of vomiting at school coming true.
- Eat meat prepared by her parents without inspecting it.
- Eat until she feels moderately full.
- Delay going to the school nurse for at least fifteen minutes after an initial feeling of sickness.
- Watch videos of babies spitting up.
- Eat three meals per day, every day, regardless of whether she feels nervous.
- Make a recipe for fake vomit.
- Watch a cartoon that has a vomiting scene.
- Watch a TV show or movie that she is avoiding because of a vomiting scene.

Here is what Esther learned: Esther learned that she could think about vomiting, see visuals of vomiting, and hear noises related to vomiting, and none of it actually caused her to vomit. Though she didn't completely eliminate her fear of vomiting, she learned to manage it in a way that didn't interfere with her life or cause her to change her behavior. She also realized that if her fear were to come true in the future and she did vomit, she would feel much more confident in her ability to cope with it compared to how she used to feel. The idea of vomiting no longer seemed as scary or as threatening to her. She also realized that while it certainly could be embarrassing if she got sick in front of her peers, it's something that others relate to, and everyone would likely move on from it.

ORGANIZING OSCAR

Oscar has specific places for all of his things, and he feels like he can't move on unless everything is in its place. Before he leaves for school, he makes his bed and hangs his towel up properly to dry. He organizes his backpack in a particular way for school, checking it several times to make sure that he has everything. He also feels like the desk in his room must be arranged a certain way before he can get started on doing homework. Oscar keeps all of his notebooks and binders from past classes in an organized system "just in case" he needs to refer back to them at some point, as he doesn't want to risk getting rid of anything that might interfere with his ability to do well in school and reach his full potential. Though he keeps them very organized, they take up a lot of space in his closet, and he knows that it probably isn't truly necessary to keep all of them.

At night, Oscar feels like he can't go to sleep without arranging his extra pillows and stuffed animals in a certain way on the floor. He wants his stuffed animals to be facing his door so that he feels extra safe at night. He worries that if he doesn't put things where they belong, he won't be able to stop thinking about it and he'll be unable to relax enough to fall asleep. Oscar is also very particular about how the clothes in his closet are hung, and he makes sure they hang neatly on hangers to avoid unnecessary wrinkles, frequently rehanging them to make sure they drape nicely. He doesn't want to look sloppy in any way when he leaves his house, and he worries that wrinkled clothing could cause other kids to judge him as lazy or disheveled.

Oscar has a meltdown if his parents rearrange anything of his, or if someone moves things from his room, as he worries that they could mess something up or break his things. Oscar also worries that if he doesn't stay organized by doing these different things, it could interfere with his ability to function at his very best.

Here is how Organizing Oscar got his *tricky, sticky, picky* brain under control:

- **Cognitive restructuring:** Oscar identified anxious thoughts and thinking traps, such as "I'll be preoccupied and unable to focus on schoolwork unless everything is in its place" (*catastrophizing, "I can't handle it"*), "I must keep everything that I have ever learned to help me reach my full academic potential" (*should statements, perfectionism*), and "Kids will judge me as lazy or disheveled if my clothes are wrinkled" (*mind-reading*). He realized that it caused him a lot of frustration to maintain these standards, so he established more balanced thoughts, such as "Things don't need to be organized perfectly in order to be functional," "It's not necessary to save all of my previous schoolwork, as I'm capable of figuring something out again that I previously learned," and "Even if I prefer organization, I can tolerate some messiness or chaos." He then practiced challenging his strict organizational efforts by engaging in ERP.
- **ERP:** Oscar started pushing back against OCD's rule that "everything had to be in its place" before he could move forward with completing tasks and activities. He practiced leaving things as they were, without fixing them, while he pursued whatever activity that he had to do. He also got rid of several items of past schoolwork. Though these tasks felt tough at first, they became much easier for him with repetition.

ORGANIZING OSCAR'S ERP CHALLENGES

- Arrange his pillows and stuffed animals in the "wrong" way during the daytime.
- Organize his backpack differently for school, switching up what items he puts in each pocket.
- Leave his bed unmade when he goes to school.
- Discard a notebook or binder from a class he did well in.
- Have his stuffed animals face away from the door at bedtime.
- Do not rehang clothes once they are on a hanger.
- Do not reorganize items on his desk.
- Wear a wrinkled shirt to school.
- Discard a notebook or binder from a past class he had difficulty in.
- Leave his room disorganized on a day that he has a test at school.

Here is what Oscar learned: Oscar realized that the standards of organization that he felt driven to follow were causing a lot of unnecessary stress for him. He found that the excessive time he spent organizing left him with less time and energy for other things, so he developed a willingness to accept imperfection in order to have time for other things that were important to him. Oscar also learned that he could still leave his house for school, focus on schoolwork, and fall asleep at night even if things weren't as his OCD told them they must be. By getting rid of past schoolwork and doing things differently, he practiced tolerating the risk that he might do something that interfered with his ability to meet his full potential. While Oscar still valued being organized, he learned that he could function even with some clutter. He learned to have a lot more flexibility and, ultimately, felt happier and much less stressed out.

ASSOCIATING ANNIE

Annie worries that other people's undesirable qualities or "vibes" will somehow rub off on her if she is in contact with them. For example, there is a girl at school who Annie thinks is a "bad kid" because she is rude to teachers and doesn't follow the rules. Annie tries to avoid this girl completely because she feels like any contact with her could emotionally contaminate her in some way. If Annie does interact with her, she feels like she has to wash her hands to rid herself of any "contamination" from their interaction. The girl recently invited Annie to her birthday party, but Annie feels way too anxious to go because she doesn't want to accidentally absorb the girl's traits and behaviors.

Annie also fears that negative vibes can spread to her from books or movies. For example, if she watches television shows, video clips, or movies or reads books that include content that she finds inappropriate, she feels like it has rubbed off on her, which makes her feel ashamed and dirty. She'll wash her hands or say a certain phrase ("I'm still Annie") to feel like she has rid herself of the icky feeling.

Annie is also a highly competitive dancer. If she is around other dancers who mess up or have bad technique, she feels like she has to do a ritual to wipe their "vibes" off her so they don't affect her performance. She sometimes counteracts the "vibes" by standing near better dancers in her class so that good vibes cancel out the bad vibes. All of this is causing a lot of anxiety for Annie, as it is difficult for her to be present in the moment since she is so focused on whether or not she could catch bad vibes.

Here is how Associating Annie got her *tricky, sticky, picky* brain under control:

- **Cognitive restructuring:** Annie recognized several anxious thoughts and thinking traps, such as "That girl at school is a bad kid" (*all-or-nothing thinking*), "It's a reflection on me if I'm around others who do bad things" (*personalization*),

"I can't be around anyone who does anything wrong" (*perfectionism*), and "If I'm around dancers with bad technique, their skills are going to rub off on me" (*magical thinking*). Annie realized that these thoughts weren't helpful or true, so she created more helpful thoughts, such as "Skills and traits are not contagious, so there's no reason to believe that I'll 'pick up' the skills or traits of others," "I can experience negative emotions without needing to eliminate them. I don't need to 'cleanse' myself to be okay," and "Feeling contaminated now does not mean I'll always feel this way. There's no evidence that this feeling will be permanent." These more balanced thoughts helped her feel more confident to engage in ERP.

- **ERP:** Annie began exposures in which she deliberately started being around people who triggered feelings of contamination, and she resisted the urge to perform compulsions to neutralize the "contamination" or "bad vibes." She started doing this over and over again to reduce the anxiety associated with them.

ASSOCIATING ANNIE'S ERP CHALLENGES

- Resist her ritual of wiping off "vibes" of dancers who she thinks have poor dance technique.
- Do not wash her hands or say her ritualistic phrase after she watches a TV show or reads a book with content that triggers her.
- Have a conversation with the girl at school and only rinse her hands with water (i.e., no soap) after the interaction.
- Have a conversation with the girl at school and do not wash her hands at all after the interaction.
- If she catches herself saying her ritualistic phrase to rid herself of icky feelings, she spoils it by recontaminating herself.
- Give high-fives to the dancers who she thinks have poor dance technique.
- Share an item with the girl at school (e.g., pencil, snack) and do not wash her hands after the interaction.
- Go to the girl's birthday party.

Here is what Annie learned: Annie learned to identify and challenge her irrational beliefs about becoming emotionally contaminated by others, as they weren't based in reality. She engaged in situations that triggered discomfort, and she saw that there was no evidence that she took on the traits that she feared in others. It also helped her make new dance friends because she allowed herself to get to know some people better who she had previously avoided. Overall, Annie realized that she could function without needing to feel "clean" or "purified" from negative emotions. This allowed her to participate more fully in school, relationships, dance, and other aspects of her life without excessive avoidance.

EXACT EZEKIAL

Ezekial gets so focused on "exactness" and accuracy that it takes his attention away from other things. He wants to follow directions accurately, so he ends up checking multiple times with his teachers to ensure he is answering the questions correctly for essays and writing assignments. He does similar things with his parents, as he'll go over his homework plan with them to make sure he is doing it right. He feels he needs to double-check these so he does not jeopardize his learning or risk his ability to try his best. Ezekial is also a singer, and his voice teacher tells him to practice his vocal exercises for fifteen minutes per day. He is very rigid about making sure he gets his exercises in for the full fifteen minutes, but not any more than that because he doesn't want to risk straining his voice.

Ever since Ezekial attended his annual check-up at the doctor earlier this year, he has been preoccupied with following health recommendations that were listed on a handout given to his parents. He is very regimented about taking his multivitamin every morning and drinking eight glasses of water per day. He is firm about brushing his teeth for two minutes, twice a day, as that is what is recommended by dentists. Ezekial is also strict about getting at least eight hours of sleep per night, exercising for sixty minutes a day, and limiting his screen time to two hours a day, as that is what is recommended for his age. He even refused to attend a recent movie theater birthday party to watch a three-hour movie, as he worried that it would be harmful to his eyes and his developing brain. He seeks to do things exactly right in order to reduce the risk of having a bad health outcome and then regretting that he could have done something more to prevent it.

Here is how Exact Ezekial got his *tricky, sticky, picky* brain under control:

- **Cognitive restructuring:** Ezekial identified anxious thoughts and thinking traps, such as "I need to be sure that I interpreted the instructions accurately" (*intolerance of uncertainty, perfectionism*), "Any more than fifteen minutes of voice practice is too much, and any less isn't good enough" (*all-or-nothing thinking*), "It'll harm my eyes and brain if I attend a three-hour movie" (*overestimation of threat*), and "I wouldn't be able to deal with the regret if I caused some sort of harm to myself" (*"I can't handle it"*). Ezekial realized that the rigid rules he was following were contributing to a great deal of unnecessary stress, so he created more balanced thoughts, such as "There are varying degrees of success, and something that's done well is still beneficial even if it's not perfect" and "It's acceptable to allow some flexibility as I work toward my goals." These new thoughts gave him the motivation to engage in ERP.

- **ERP:** Ezekial learned to recognize and challenge when he was following overly strict rules or engaging in all-or-nothing thinking. He engaged in exposures in which he gradually did things differently or inexactly to practice applying a "good enough" standard. He practiced allowing a reasonable degree of risk and accepted uncertainty without getting reassurance.

EXACT EZEKIAL'S EXPOSURE ERP CHALLENGES

- Skip his multivitamin one morning.
- Watch a movie that is three hours long.
- Brush his teeth for one minute.
- Get seven hours of sleep one night.
- Practice his vocal exercises for eighteen minutes (instead of fifteen) during the day.
- Drink six glasses of water per day (instead of eight).
- Practice his vocal exercises for ten minutes during the day.
- Complete a writing assignment without seeking reassurance from his parents or teachers about the directions.
- Skip one day of vocal exercises.

Here is what Ezekial learned: Ezekial learned to recognize extreme thought patterns and replace them with more balanced perspectives. He learned to embrace flexibility and avoid unnecessarily strict rules and overly harsh judgments of himself. He developed a much healthier perspective rather than seeing things in only extremes, and this allowed him to set more realistic and attainable goals.

NEED-TO-KNOW NANCY

Nancy feels a strong need to know about a variety of things, and she has associated anxiousness if she thinks she has missed something. She worries that it could have been important or that she'll always be stuck wondering whether she missed anything. With schoolwork, she reads things over and over in her textbooks because she doubts whether she understood something fully or is worried that she zoned out and missed something. When she watches TV, she often rewinds the show if she can't clearly hear what a character says, in case it is something that will be important to understand the plot. Nancy will also ask her parents and friends to repeat things if she doesn't hear what they say, as she doesn't want to always be wondering what it was and whether it could have changed the course of her life in some way.

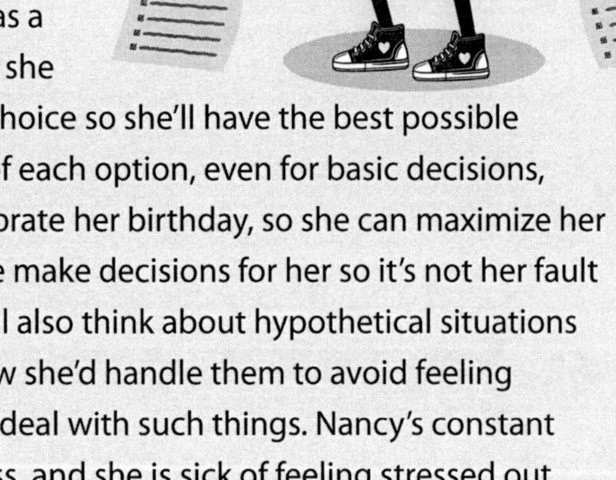

Nancy also feels like she needs to have the best possible experience with whatever she is doing. She goes over things in her head and makes lists to make sure she doesn't forget them. She has a very difficult time making decisions because she obsesses about making the "right" or "best" choice so she'll have the best possible outcome. She'll consider the pros and cons of each option, even for basic decisions, such as what sneakers to buy or how to celebrate her birthday, so she can maximize her experience. Sometimes she lets other people make decisions for her so it's not her fault if something doesn't turn out well. Nancy will also think about hypothetical situations that could happen in the future and plan how she'd handle them to avoid feeling anxious or unprepared if she actually had to deal with such things. Nancy's constant overthinking takes a big toll on her happiness, and she is sick of feeling stressed out so often.

Here is how Need-to-Know Nancy got her *tricky, sticky, picky* brain under control:

- **Cognitive restructuring:** Nancy identified anxious thoughts and thinking traps, such as "I can't handle not knowing whether or not I missed something. What if it bothers me forever?" (*catastrophizing*, *"I can't handle it"*), "It could change the course of my life in some way if I missed something important" (*intolerance of uncertainty, overestimating threat*), and "I must do everything I can to make sure I'm making the right decision" (*should statements, perfectionism*). Nancy realized that even after her pursuit to figure out answers, new questions or doubts continued to arise about other things. She realized that this pattern wasn't serving her well, so she created more balanced thoughts, such as "I can make decisions with a reasonable amount of information. I can then handle the consequences of my decisions, even if they don't turn out as expected" and "It's unrealistic to expect to know everything perfectly. It's okay to have gaps in knowledge. I can make informed choices without needing complete information." These new thoughts helped her start challenging herself through ERP.

- **ERP:** Nancy engaged in exercises in which she purposely aimed to leave her "need to know" feeling unsatisfied. Specifically, she engaged in exposures that involved doing things only once and moving forward even if she felt unsure about whatever the content was. By reducing checking and reassurance-seeking rituals, she took risks that she might miss something, and she accepted the possibility that it could impact her in some way.

NEED-TO-KNOW NANCY'S ERP CHALLENGES

- Watch a TV show and do not rewind at all.
- Make a decision at an ice cream store within one minute.
- Read a history chapter without any rereading.
- Read a science or math chapter without any rereading.
- Do not have her friends repeat what they said.
- Do not have her parents repeat what they said.
- Within five minutes of reviewing the menu at a restaurant, make a decision about what to order.
- Make a decision about her birthday party within one hour of researching places to have the party.
- Within thirty minutes of visiting a shoe store, make a decision about what sneakers to purchase.

Here is what Nancy learned: Nancy learned that she could move forward even if she didn't have a complete understanding of the questions that triggered her anxiety. Though she worried that this uncertainty would plague her forever, she was surprised to see that this fear faded over time. She also learned that she could make thoughtful decisions in a shorter amount of time, and she could have confidence in her decision-making without needing others to give her confirmation. Instead of putting so much pressure on herself to feel completely confident that she made the "right" or "best" decision, she aimed to make thoughtful decisions without labeling decisions as "good" or "bad." Ultimately, she realized that it was more meaningful to her to spend time on things that she valued rather than spend unnecessary time on compulsions to satisfy her "need to know."

SUPERSTITIOUS SOLOMON

Solomon worries a lot about accidentally doing something that will cause bad luck, so he avoids specific numbers (six and thirteen), colors (red and black), and other things (black cats and ladders) that he believes are unlucky. Whenever he has a thought about something bad happening, he'll also "knock on wood" to try to prevent it. If he ends on a bad thought when he is doing something, he'll continue doing the activity until he ends on a neutral or positive thought, or else he worries that something bad will happen.

Solomon takes baseball very seriously and plays on a travel team, and he has also developed a variety of superstitious rituals that he thinks are tied to him playing well. For example, he eats the same breakfast and lunch on game days, which can sometimes be difficult to coordinate, particularly if he is traveling. He also gets very upset if he doesn't have his lucky socks on game days, and he won't wash his uniform after a win. Solomon is his team's pitcher, and he feels like he needs to kiss the baseball before every pitch or else the batter will hit a homerun. Unfortunately, these superstitious rituals take away from his enjoyment of his favorite sport.

Here is how Superstitious Solomon got his *tricky, sticky, picky* brain under control:

- **Cognitive restructuring:** Solomon recognized his anxious thoughts and thinking traps, such as "Something bad will happen if I use certain numbers or colors" (*magical thinking*), "I must follow the same pregame rituals on game days, such as eating the same breakfast and lunch, wearing my lucky socks, and kissing the ball before every pitch" (*repetitive thinking, perfectionism*), and "Something bad will happen if I walk under a ladder, walk near a black cat, or don't knock on wood" (*magical thinking*). He then established healthier, more balanced ways of thinking, including "There's no evidence of a logical connection between these random actions and the outcome" and "Superstitions give me the illusion of control, but there's no scientific evidence that luck is connected to what I wear or do." These new thoughts helped give Solomon the willingness to challenge his superstitious rituals through ERP.
- **ERP:** Solomon started doing things differently than what his OCD told him to do. Specifically, he used numbers and colors that he had avoided due to superstitious fears, and he also started confronting other fears without knocking on wood. He varied up his pregame activities so that he didn't always do and wear the same things on game days. He also stopped neutralizing bad thoughts and counteracting them with positive thoughts.

SUPERSTITIOUS SOLOMON'S ERP CHALLENGES

- Eat thirteen pretzels.
- Do not kiss the baseball before each pitch.
- Wear black or red clothing to an important event.
- Eat a different breakfast on the day of his baseball game.
- Do as many things using the number six as possible in one day.
- End on a bad thought (instead of a neutral or positive thought) while doing something of small importance.
- Do not knock on wood if he has a thought about something bad happening.
- Wash his baseball uniform after a win.
- Do experiments in which he writes about bad things happening, such as "I want ___________ to happen today." See if those things then come true.
- End on a bad thought while doing something of high importance.

Here is what Solomon learned: Solomon learned that there was no actual basis to the superstitions that he had been following. Initially, he was initially hesitant to take the risk of challenging OCD because he worried that it would cause bad luck or have a negative impact on his baseball game. However, by eliminating all of the OCD-related rituals, it actually strengthened his focus and discipline in baseball, as he was less preoccupied with OCD thoughts and needing to do things a certain way. Solomon was able to be much more present rather than living with so much anxiety and fear.

DISGUSTED DAMIAN

Damian becomes extremely upset by things he finds to be "disgusting." He gets grossed out if he is around people who are doing things that he finds to be disgusting, such as wiping their nose with their hands (instead of a tissue) or picking their nose. He isn't afraid of the germs—he just finds the behavior to be completely repulsive and off-putting, and he often ends up saying something unkind to the person about how gross it is and asking them to wash their hands, which he then feels bad about afterward.

Damian also can't stand being around animal poop, as he thinks it is completely disgusting. This started to bother him when his dog got sick and pooped all over the house. Ever since, he washes his hands a lot after he plays with his dog, as he worries that some of the poop from the dog's butt could somehow have spread to other parts of his body, like his paws or his face. Damian thinks this would be super gross. Sometimes he avoids his dog altogether because he gets so anxious about washing his hands in case he may have touched poop particles without realizing it. He also stopped taking his dog on walks, as he doesn't want to even see his dog's poop or have to pick it up. Damian also avoids riding his bike around his neighborhood with friends because he is so worried that he'll end up seeing poop from dogs or other animals. This causes him to miss out on time with his friends.

Additionally, Damian gets bothered with feeling "dirty," so he gets preoccupied with separating things that he perceives to be "clean" from items he considers to be "dirty." He worries that if he doesn't separate them, everything he touched would eventually become "dirty" through cross-contamination, and that feels incredibly "gross" and irreparable to him. He specifically puts in a lot of effort to keep his room as his clean and safe space. If he goes outside his house, he changes his clothes before he enters his room so he can prevent his room from being contaminated by outside germs. Further, Damian has a nightly ritual before bedtime in which he uses the bathroom, takes a shower, and then doesn't leave his room again, since he doesn't want to risk getting into his bed with any germs that could contaminate it and cause it to become "dirty."

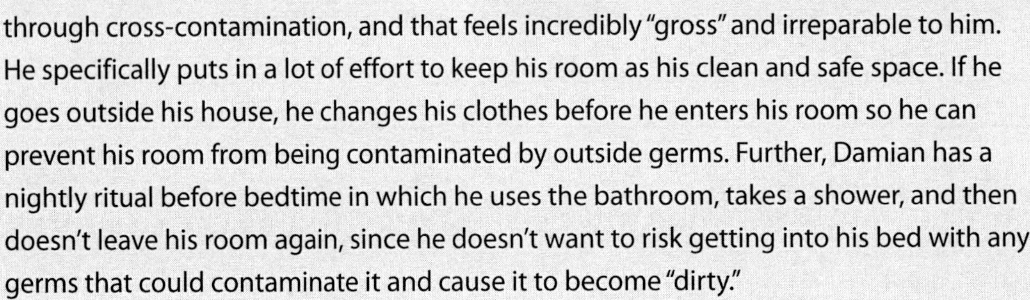

Here is how Disgusted Damian got his *tricky, sticky, picky* brain under control:

- **Cognitive restructuring:** Damian recognized the presence of anxious thoughts and thinking traps, such as "I can't tolerate feeling grossed out or dirty" (*catastrophizing, "I can't handle it"*), "People should never use their hands to wipe their nose" (*should statements*), "Things are either clean or dirty" (*all-or-nothing thinking*), and "If I feel disgusted, I can't enjoy the rest of my day" (*negative glasses*). He realized that these thoughts weren't allowing him to enjoy his life as much as he wanted, so he established more balanced thoughts, such as "I can feel disgusted but still safely handle dog poop without having to avoid it or react excessively," "Disgust is just a feeling and not an indication of danger," and "I can feel dirty without having to act on it and still be okay." He then used these new thoughts as motivation to engage in ERP.
- **ERP:** Damian's exposure challenges focused on reducing avoidance and gradually confronting the things that provoked feelings of disgust. He practiced noticing these feelings without reacting to them and learned to sit with the discomfort. Damian also focused on the ways in which reducing compulsions aligned with

his goals (e.g., bike riding, spending time with his dog) and his overall well-being. He started tolerating feeling "dirty" as well, and he'd keep engaging with daily activities even if he felt "dirty." Further, Damian began doing exposures that challenged OCD's rules about separating things that are "clean" versus "dirty." Instead of keeping these items separate, he gradually started to cross-contaminate them.

DISGUSTED DAMIAN'S ERP CHALLENGES

- Ride his bicycle around the neighborhood with friends. Do not alter his path if he sees animal poop.
- Rinse his hands with just water (i.e., no soap) after playing with his dog.
- Wear one item of "outside" clothing inside his home.
- Wear an entire outfit of "outside" clothing inside his home.
- Invite his friends over for pizza night. If a friend does something gross (e.g., wipes their nose with their hand and doesn't wash after), resist commenting about it or asking them to wash their hands.
- Play soccer at the park, despite the potential that he may come across animal poop.
- Do not wash his hands at all after playing with his dog.
- Wear one item of "outside" clothing while sitting on his bed.
- Tag along with his parents while they walk the dog.
- Walk the dog and wear gloves when picking up dog poop.
- Go to the dog park and observe dogs going poop.
- Wear an entire outfit of "outside" clothing while sitting on his bed.
- Let his dog sleep in bed with him.

Here is what Damian learned: Damian learned that the feeling of disgust is tolerable and that he could experience disgust without needing to react or do compulsions to make the feeling go away. By repetitively facing disgust triggers, they became less emotionally intense to deal with, which weakened their power over him. Damian also learned that he could tolerate "feeling dirty," and over time, it became less upsetting to him. He stopped keeping track of what was "clean" and what was "dirty," and he was surprised to see that it got easier once he started cross-contaminating things, as he was able to live his life with a lot less stress since he was no longer so preoccupied with these concerns.

OMINOUS OLIVIA

Olivia focuses a lot on death and related omens. She has been taught that the number four is taboo because her culture associates it with death, so she avoids doing anything in fours. Her culture's traditional color of mourning is white, so white is often worn at funerals. However, Olivia now refuses to wear white at other times because she worries that it could "bring on death" to herself or her loved ones. Olivia also learned that her culture considers it taboo to give clocks as gifts because they're associated with the end of life. Unfortunately, this has caused Olivia to feel really anxious around clocks in general, so she'll avoid looking at them.

In Olivia's culture, feet are considered to be the dirtiest part of the body, so it's considered disrespectful to point one's feet at anyone or anything sacred (e.g., a temple). Olivia has taken this to the extreme, and she is constantly thinking about the direction that her feet are pointing and readjusting them to make sure she isn't doing anything that would be offensive. In Olivia's culture, it's also considered rude for men and women to kiss, hug, or hold hands in public. Olivia is therefore constantly worried that she'll be around other people who do this, due to concerns about what it might say about her. She asks her parents if anyone will be doing those things when they go out in public, and she wants confirmation that they can leave the place if she sees such behaviors.

Here is how Ominous Olivia got her *tricky, sticky, picky* brain under control:

- **Cognitive restructuring:** Olivia identified anxious thoughts and thinking traps, such as "I can't do anything in fours" (*all-or-nothing thinking*), "If I wear white, it'll bring on death to my loved ones" (*magical thinking*), "I'm doing something wrong if I'm around men and women who show affection to each other" (*inflated responsibility*), and "My feet should always be aligned appropriately" (*should statements*). She realized that she had an overly strict standard for adhering to her culture's practices that was actually interfering with her appreciation of her culture, so she strived to find a healthier balance by engaging in ERP.
- **ERP:** Since Olivia realized that a lot of her avoidance was excessive, she engaged in exposures in which she confronted a lot of the situations that she was avoiding. She also consulted with a cultural leader to determine the guidelines that others in her culture were following; that way, she could stop taking these practices to the extreme. This helped her engage in a lot more ERP exercises, such as decreasing reassurance, wearing white, using the number four, and walking without monitoring the direction of her feet.

OMINOUS OLIVIA'S ERP CHALLENGES

- Draw a picture of a clock.
- Do not adjust the direction of her feet while outside during gym class.
- Wear one piece of white clothing on a regular school day.
- Wear all white clothing on a regular school day.
- Watch a TV show or movie that shows males and females exhibiting physical affection (e.g., holding hands, hugging, kissing).
- Do not adjust the direction of her feet while in the classroom at school.
- When she goes out of the house, do not get reassurance from her parents about whether people there will be holding hands romantically.
- Wear white on a special day, like a holiday.
- Go to a home goods store and walk up and down the clock aisle.
- Stay present in a situation where people are holding hands romantically.
- Keep a clock in her bedroom.

Here is what Olivia learned: Olivia learned that she could still do what is important to her, which is to observe her culture's practices, without abiding by OCD's rules. She realized that many of the rules she was living by were actually OCD rules that were trying to masquerade as rules of her culture. With this new understanding, she was able to respect her culture without being overly strict. Once she stopped being bossed around by OCD, she was able to gain a lot more meaning and purpose through participating in her cultural practices.

TABOO TIMMY

Timmy gets thoughts throughout the day that he thinks are weird or inappropriate. For example, he might have a thought about his family and friends being naked, or their private parts, which bothers him a lot. He'll also wonder, "Did I like that thought?" and try to reassure himself that he felt gross in response to the thoughts. When Timmy has these kinds of thoughts, he swiftly shakes his head from side to side to try to erase them from his brain. He feels embarrassed to have these thoughts and wonders if other people can tell when he thinks them.

Timmy also gets thoughts about people kissing, which he thinks is gross. If he sees people kiss on a TV show, he'll avoid watching that show again, as he doesn't like the image to be in his head and doesn't want others to think he likes it.

Timmy also worries that he may have looked at someone's private parts, which then makes him feel weird and disgusted with himself. If he has this worry, he'll then try to think back and analyze whether or not he looked at the person there, and whether looking there was an accident or on purpose. Since Timmy doesn't want to offend anyone or do anything inappropriate, he focuses extra hard to make sure he looks people in the eyes. All of these thoughts make Timmy feel ashamed, upset, and embarrassed.

Here is how Taboo Timmy got his *tricky, sticky, picky* brain under control:

- **Cognitive restructuring:** Timmy identified anxious thoughts and thinking traps, such as "It must say something about me that I have these weird thoughts" (*overimportance of thoughts*), "I need to erase any inappropriate thoughts from my brain" (*need to control thoughts*), and "I need to know whether I looked at their private parts on purpose" (*intolerance of uncertainty*). Timmy checked the facts and created more balanced thoughts, such as "Thoughts are just thoughts. Having a thought doesn't mean that I want to act on it," "Regardless of whatever thoughts pop into my head, I can control my behavior and how much attention I give to them," and "My values and actions are what matter, not the thoughts that come into my mind." These new thoughts helped Timmy take the risk of challenging what OCD was telling him to do, which he did through ERP.
- **ERP:** Timmy engaged in exposures in which he intentionally did things that triggered inappropriate thoughts and then resisted the urge to do compulsions to cancel out the thought or reassure himself. He practiced allowing the thoughts to be present and stopped judging himself for having them.

TABOO TIMMY'S ERP CHALLENGES

- Draw a picture of people kissing.
- Read an age-appropriate book about where babies come from.
- Let gross thoughts be present without doing anything in response to "erase" them.
- Let gross thoughts be present while he is around other people.
- Watch a TV show or movie with a scene in which people kiss.
- Purposely look at people in a clothing catalog and resist rituals if taboo thoughts come up.
- Refrain from trying to answer OCD's questions, such as whether or not he liked a taboo thought or if he meant to look at someone's privates.

Here is what Timmy learned: Timmy learned to tolerate the discomfort of intrusive thoughts without needing to neutralize them, which ultimately reduced the power that these thoughts were holding over him. He learned to reframe intrusive thoughts as simply thoughts rather than reflections of his true self. Timmy also learned to treat himself with kindness instead of shame.

SUDDENLY SOPHIE

Sophie has always been a great student and good kid. She is super social and has always enjoyed spending time with her friends. However, Sophie was recently out of school with the flu and had a sore throat for a whole week. Two weeks after she returned to school, she started to show extreme anxiety and moodiness. Her parents described her as being a "different kid" overnight, as if a switch flipped. She was suddenly doing things repetitively, such as going up and down the stairs and opening and closing drawers, until she got a feeling that it was "just right." Her parents also noticed that she was suddenly getting sloppy with her schoolwork and acting much younger than before. Her writing wasn't as neat as it used to be, and she wasn't as coordinated when she played soccer, though that was never a problem previously.

Sophie began to wash her hands excessively, and she'd count while washing to ensure she washed "enough." If someone disrupted her, she'd yell at them and feel like she had to start her handwashing all over. Sophie also began avoiding soccer practice and National Honor Society meetings because she was afraid that she'd catch germs from peers. She obsessed about germs at home, such as wondering if her parents washed their hands before making dinner or if her siblings took off their shoes inside the house. These things never seemed to bother Sophie before, and her parents started to feel like they were walking on eggshells around her. In turn, they started to wash their own hands a lot, reassured her that they were clean, and made a new house rule that no one could wear shoes in the house. All of this was to keep the peace in the home and try to prevent Sophie's anxiety from being triggered. No one could understand why Sophie was suddenly so distraught about germs, but it had created a lot of stress within the home.

Sophie's parents eventually reached out to a doctor to discuss her symptoms, and after additional testing, they learned that Sophie had developed PANDAS in response to a recent strep infection—likely around the same time she had the flu. They were relieved to have a diagnosis that explained the sudden change in their daughter and began pursuing treatment to help her recover.

Here is how Suddenly Sophie got her *tricky, sticky, picky* brain under control:

- **Cognitive restructuring:** Sophie identified anxious thoughts and thinking traps, such as "I can't move on unless things feel 'just right'" (*"I can't handle it," catastrophizing*), "If I am disrupted while handwashing, I have to start over, as otherwise it doesn't count" (*all-or-nothing thinking*), and "I can't eat unless I know for sure that my parents washed their hands before cooking" (*intolerance of uncertainty*). Sophie collected evidence for and against her beliefs, which helped her develop more balanced thoughts, such as "I never used to confirm that my parents washed their hands before cooking, and I was fine then, so I'll probably be fine this time," "I don't need to wash perfectly in order for things to be acceptable and safe," and "I can tolerate feeling uncomfortable without having to do anything about it." Sophie then used these new thoughts as motivation to take the risk and face her fears with ERP.
- **ERP:** Sophie started to do exposures in which she practiced completing daily tasks (e.g., using the stairs, washing her hands, eating) the same way she did *before* the sudden onset of OCD symptoms. She purposely did tasks differently or the opposite of what OCD wanted her to do.
- **Medication:** Doctors prescribed Sophie antibiotic medication that she took for a period of two weeks to help treat her underlying infection. They then monitored her to determine whether they should give her infusions to further help her body fight off any infections.

SUDDENLY SOPHIE'S ERP CHALLENGES

- Leave a drawer open in a way that "feels wrong."
- Limit her handwashing to sixty seconds with soap.
- Attend a National Honor Society meeting and sit at a desk in the middle of her peers.
- Do not ask her parents if they washed their hands before preparing food.
- Walk up or down the stairs in a way that feels "wrong."
- Limit her handwashing to thirty seconds with soap.
- Limit her handwashing to thirty seconds without soap.
- Attend soccer practice and give high-fives to her teammates without washing her hands after.
- Family members wear shoes in the common areas of the house.

Note: In addition to using these strategies, remember that any time there is a sudden and dramatic onset of symptoms like Sophie experienced, it is helpful to discuss these symptoms with a medical doctor to determine whether they reflect PANS or PANDAS. If so, certain medicines or medical treatments may be helpful to fight back against OCD.

Here is what Sophie learned: Sophie learned that while her sudden symptoms may have been triggered by an autoimmune response, she could still exert power over them. By practicing ERP strategies, she gained confidence that she could manage her symptoms. She also worked with her family to identify early signs of flare-ups so she could intervene with skills as soon as possible, and she aimed to have self-compassion when these setbacks occurred.

Now that you've met some of my friends with OCD, you can see many different ways that OCD can show up. Despite what some people may say, no OCD symptoms are easier or better than others—they all can cause a ton of anxiety and distress, and they all get in the way of living your life. Hopefully, this chapter helped you understand that you can use the same basic strategies to fight back against any symptom of OCD, regardless of the ways in which it picks on you.

The next chapter talks about the importance of living a life that is meaningful instead of allowing OCD to define who you are or what you do. It'll also discuss tips for navigating some of the common issues that may arise when you are living life with OCD.

CHAPTER 13

Living Life with a *Tricky, Sticky, Picky* Brain

In addition to learning how to manage OCD symptoms, there are many other questions that may come up as you go through life with OCD. This includes questions like "Should I tell people about my diagnosis?" "What information should I share?" How do I deal with stigma?" and "Will I be able to live a normal life?" The goal of this chapter is to address many of these questions and help you develop goals to live a happy, meaningful life.

Deciding Whether to Tell People About Your OCD

It's a personal decision whether you choose to tell others about your OCD. For example, what do you think about telling your extended family members, like aunts, uncles, cousins, and grandparents? Are you worried they might not be understanding or take it seriously? What about sharing your OCD diagnosis with close friends? If you do tell friends, what specifically will you say? Perhaps you have concerns about whether your friends will think you're weird or still want to be your friend. Maybe you're concerned they'll share your personal information with others. Since OCD is a very misunderstood disorder, it is important to be thoughtful about how and what you share with others. When deciding whether or not to tell others, here are some questions to ask yourself:

- Can you identify any potential benefits of telling others about your OCD?
- If you are having a tough time because of OCD, could sharing your experiences lessen the burden you are carrying since others may be understanding and offer support?
- Do you feel like you're in a good place to handle whatever response you get? What if you feel rejected or judged? Could you take that on at this time?

- Will it serve a purpose to share that you have OCD? For example, will it help you access support, reduce stigma, practice self-acceptance, reduce the pressure of "hiding" symptoms, or help others understand your avoidance behaviors?
- Are you concerned that if you share that you have OCD, you'll be discriminated against or looked at differently by your culture or religious community?

Whom to Share It With

In addition to asking yourself the previous questions, you'll want to decide whom to tell about your OCD. For example, you may choose to talk about your *tricky, sticky, picky* brain with close friends but not with peers who don't know you too well. Here are some things to consider when making a decision:

- **Family:** Is it important for some family members to know about your OCD so that they can better support you? Or are you concerned that some family members may be judgmental? Maybe you have a sibling and are worried that they'll pick on you for it. If you do share your diagnosis with family members, it's often helpful to have a parent involved in this discussion.
- **Friends:** We all have different kinds of friends, ranging from best friends who know us well to acquaintances who know just a little bit about us. You might have some friends you can talk to about tough things and others you just have fun or play sports with. If you do tell your friends about your OCD, it's often best to start with a close friend whom you can trust. That way, you can use that initial conversation to help guide later conversations with others.
- **Peers:** Do you want all your peers to know about your OCD? If so, think about *why* you feel that way. Remember that OCD isn't your whole identity, so you might not want to risk having people define you based on that, especially your peers you don't know well. It also may not make sense to share something personal with people who aren't invested in learning more about it. At the same time, there are certainly a lot of advantages to being open about your OCD. For example, maybe your classmates have picked up on your compulsions, and by telling them all at once, you hope that their questions stop. Maybe by sharing something personal that you're going through, it will provide an opportunity to help someone else or allow you to connect with someone you wouldn't have otherwise connected with.
- **Teachers and school staff:** Although you may have concerns that teachers will think differently about you if your share your OCD diagnosis, it can be helpful to let them know in case you need some extra support in place with academics. In

fact, there are several laws in the United States that require schools to provide you with extra support (called *accommodations*) if you have a condition like OCD that is causing academic problems. For example, if it takes you longer to complete schoolwork or tests because of your compulsions, accommodations might include extended time on tests or in-class work, a quiet or distraction-free environment for test-taking, note-taking help, a reduced course load, or extra breaks as needed. Any accommodations can be individualized based on your specific OCD symptoms.

At the same time, it is important to know that many accommodations for OCD may cause your symptoms to stick around. For instance, if you are given an accommodation of extra time on tests because you excessively rewrite your answers and don't finish tests on time, the accommodation may cause you to be less motivated to challenge your rewriting compulsion since there would be less pressure to do so. Therefore, it's best to make sure that any accommodations for OCD are temporary and that you are still doing ERP treatment to reduce or eliminate your rituals.

- **Public:** There's a lot to think about when you consider sharing your personal information in public spaces, such as social media. Anything you post online can often be shared widely, and this can lead to both positive and negative consequences. For example, you might challenge misconceptions about OCD or combat stigma by sharing your experiences. You might also be able to connect with kids who relate to you, which can help you (and them) feel less alone.

  On the other hand, publicly sharing your personal information might lead you to receive hurtful comments online from people who don't understand OCD. In addition, although you might post something at age thirteen, you may feel differently about having your personal information on the internet when you eventually apply to colleges or jobs. Remember that everything you post online will have a digital footprint forever. Even if you later decide to take down a post or retract a message, this isn't always doable. Ultimately, it's important to be thoughtful about anything you put online or in writing, and if possible, consult a trusted adult to help you think through such decisions.

What to Share

If you do decide to talk about your OCD, there's a wide range of information that you can choose to share with others. Perhaps you just share that you have OCD and give general information about the disorder, or you might decide to share specifics about your symptoms. I recommend sharing a little bit at a time so you can see how others respond to what you tell them. If they seem supportive and caring, you can tell them more by talking about your specific worries and rituals—but only if you feel comfortable and want to. Since some aspects of your OCD may feel more personal than others, you may also decide to share some things but not others. Remember that this is all your choice. If someone asks for details that you do not want to share, just tell them that you aren't comfortable discussing specifics at this time.

Chances are that if you do share your diagnosis, people are going to ask how they can help you. However, it may be that you don't want their help. Maybe you just want them to listen to your story and then treat you exactly the same. If so, it is helpful to let these people know that you aren't looking for their input, their advice, or for them to be your therapist. You just want them to listen and support you. However, if you do want them to play a more active role in helping you, give them ideas! Perhaps you'd like for them to distract you when you're anxious by encouraging a fun activity. Maybe you'd like to find a way to face an OCD challenge with them by your side. Or maybe you'd like to plan something special you can do together as a reward for conquering something difficult. It's a good idea to give some thought to this in case it comes up when you talk to loved ones about your OCD.

Either way, let others know what to do with any information you share with them. If you want your friends to keep things just between you and them, make sure that is clear to them so they don't go and share your personal matters with others. Here is a sample script of how you might share this information with a friend:

You: Hey [*friend's name*], there's something I want to tell you about me.

Friend: What is it?

You: Well, sometimes it is a bit more difficult for me to do certain things. Or I might do things a bit differently than others. It's because I have something called OCD, which stands for obsessive-compulsive disorder. Because of this, my brain tells me that I have to do certain things, even if I don't really want to. If I don't do what it tells me, I often feel really upset or worried.

Friend: Oh, what do you mean exactly?

You: Sometimes my brain makes me feel worried or anxious if things aren't just right, or it tells me that I have to do certain routines to feel better, even when I know they might not make sense.

Friend: That sounds tough. Are you okay?

You: Yes, thank you. I'm learning strategies to handle it better, and I also have family and doctors who help me.

Friend: Is there anything I can do to help?

You: Just continue to be my friend and understand that I might sometimes need a little extra time to do things, or I might seem a bit worried about certain things. Maybe just be patient with me if I'm having a tough day.

Friend: Oh, okay. Let me know if there's anything else I can do to help.

You: I will. I appreciate you listening. If you ever have questions about it, just let me know.

If you have chosen to talk about your OCD with close friends or family members, there are a lot of resources you can use to help them better understand what you're going through. You can direct them to the International OCD Foundation (www.iocdf.org) or give them an article on OCD. Maybe you watch an OCD documentary or movie with them, or attend an OCD awareness event and ask them to join you. Any of these things can be used as starting points!

Be Prepared for Different Responses

Although it's likely that good friends and family members will be supportive when you share your experiences with them, it's also possible that you'll get responses that are different from what you were expecting. For example, in rare cases, they might respond with a joke or by making fun of you, in which case you can say, "This is something that is really difficult for me. It isn't a joke, and if you care about me, you'll realize that it's not something to make fun of. If you're open to learning more about what OCD is really like, then we can talk more about it." At other times, they might respond insensitively, but with good intentions, in which case it's worth sharing more about what OCD is really like so they can better support you. However, your friends and family don't need to be experts in OCD to be a source of support or understanding for you.

There is also a chance that people will respond by saying, "I have OCD too" or "My family member has OCD." If so, this can be an opportunity to connect with them and share the difficulties you have both experienced. However, if it's clear that they're talking about wanting to do things a certain way out of preference or habit—and not because they have real OCD symptoms—this is an opportunity for you to highlight the differences between the two. For example, you might respond by saying something like "It sounds like you have some things that you prefer to do a certain way. The difference for me is that it doesn't feel like a choice to me. I feel like I *have* to do whatever my OCD wants me to do, even though I don't want to do it. If I don't do what OCD wants, I get incredibly scared and anxious, and the fear consumes me to the point that I feel like I can't do anything else." Keep in mind that when people make comments like "I have OCD too"—when they don't actually have OCD—they are probably just trying to relate to you, not upset you. Sometimes people make these comments because there are a lot of myths and stereotypes about OCD that do not reflect what it is really like. Therefore, it can be helpful to use these discussions as opportunities to help educate others about OCD.

Staying Focused on Your Goals

Many kids with OCD already feel different, so it's understandable if you're wondering whether you'll be able to have the kind of life you want and fulfill your goals for the future. This is especially the case if your OCD makes it difficult to do many basic daily tasks, like showering, eating, doing chores, and getting dressed. You might have doubts about whether you'll be able to handle it all as you get older. Here are some common worries you (and other kids) might have:

- Will I get through school?
- Will I go to college? Could I go somewhere away from home?
- Will I be able to get a job?
- Am I going to be able to take care of myself (e.g., drive, cook, clean)?
- Can I be happy?
- Will I be successful?
- Can I find someone to accept me and love me?
- Will I ever get married or have kids?

Though there's no crystal ball to tell us what will happen in the future, it's important to emphasize that OCD does not need to hold you back from pursuing your goals in life. It can be difficult to believe this when you are in the middle of a bad OCD episode, but it is possible to live a happy, healthy, and successful life despite having OCD. With the tools you have learned, you can keep OCD in check so it doesn't cause you to miss out on whatever is important to you. Then you can begin setting goals that you'd like to achieve in life, whatever they may be—whether it's running for class president, studying to be a veterinarian, or making the basketball team. You can achieve these goals when you have the attitude and mindset that you won't let OCD stop you.

What Are Your Goals?

When setting goals, it's helpful to be detailed and specific (as opposed to vague and overly general) so you can maximize your chances of success. One framework to set effective goals is to use the acronym SMART, which stands for the following:

- **Specific:** Clearly define what you want to accomplish and why it's important.
- **Measurable:** Determine how you will measure your progress and whether you've met your goal.
- **Achievable:** Make sure you have the necessary skills and resources to achieve your goal. If you don't, think about how you could attain them.
- **Relevant:** Ensure this specific goal is aligned with your broader objectives. Does it make sense in terms of your broader goals?
- **Timebound:** Set reasonable deadlines to complete your goal.

For example, let's say your goal is to be more social this school year. You can turn this into a SMART goal in the following way:

- **Specific:** Join at least one club or extracurricular activity that aligns with your interests, and attend a school social event, like a sports game or a dance. Start a conversation with at least one new person per week. Make plans with friends at least two times per month.
- **Measurable:** Track the number of people you talk to each week and the number of social events you attend.
- **Achievable:** Begin with small steps, such as saying hello to a peer, giving someone a compliment, or asking someone if they need help.
- **Relevant:** Being social is important at school since you need to be able to speak up in class, give presentations, and connect with your peers for group projects. Therefore, this goal will allow you to build confidence and have a more enjoyable school experience.
- **Timebound:**
  - **First two weeks:** Introduce yourself to at least five new people and attend one school event.
  - **First month:** Join a club or extracurricular activity to consistently engage with peers.
  - **End of school year:** Build and maintain at least three meaningful friendships.

Now it's your turn. Think of some broad goals you want to achieve in life and write them down here.

1. ______________________________

____

2. ______________________________

____

3. ______________________________

____

4. ______________________________

____

5. ______________________________

____

Now that you have brainstormed some goals, how can you make sure that these goals are SMART? In other words, break each goal into smaller, more manageable tasks that will help you achieve your goal.

Goal #1: ______________________________

SMART Goal:

Specific: ______________________________

____

Measurable: ______________________________

____

Achievable: ______________________________

____

Relevant: ______________________________

____

Timebound: ______________________________

____

Are there any obstacles that could get in the way of you reaching this goal? Do you have any specific worries or fears? Write them down and then brainstorm what you could do to overcome them.

____

____

____

____

____

____

Goal #2: ______________________________

SMART Goal:

Specific: ______________________________

____

Measurable: ______________________________

____

Achievable: ______________________________

____

Relevant: ______________________________

____

Timebound: ______________________________

____

Are there any obstacles that could get in the way of you reaching this goal? Do you have any specific worries or fears? Write them down and then brainstorm what you could do to overcome them.

____

____

____

____

____

____

Goal #3: ____________________

SMART Goal:

Specific: ____________________

____

Measurable: ____________________

____

Achievable: ____________________

____

Relevant: ____________________

____

Timebound: ____________________

____

Are there any obstacles that could get in the way of you reaching this goal? Do you have any specific worries or fears? Write them down and then brainstorm what you could do to overcome them.

____

____

____

____

____

____

Goal #4: ____________________

SMART Goal:

Specific: ____________________

____

Measurable: ____________________

____

Achievable: ____________________

____

Relevant: ____

____

Timebound: ____

____

Are there any obstacles that could get in the way of you reaching this goal? Do you have any specific worries or fears? Write them down and then brainstorm what you could do to overcome them.

____

____

____

____

____

____

This chapter covered many important topics that come up in relation to living life with OCD. Hopefully, it helped you feel even more confident in your ability to work through different questions and situations that may come up along the way. In the next chapter, you will hear from *real* kids who have overcome their OCD. Though it is a condition that needs to be managed, it doesn't need to hold you back from doing what matters to you, living purposefully, and achieving your goals!

CHAPTER 14

Advice from *Real Kids* Who Have Been There

This chapter includes advice, tips, and words of encouragement from *real kids* who have worked to overcome OCD. The hope is that this will help inspire you to put in the work to challenge your OCD!

BRONSON, AGE 11

1. **Please share a bit about your experience with OCD.**

   My OCD started when I was eight or nine years old. I am not sure why OCD picked on me, but I am thinking it has to do with me having anxiety. My OCD would make me do things like praying, standing up and down, and touching doorknobs multiple times. I would worry about myself dying if I did not do a certain compulsion. If I did not pray multiple times a day, I thought I could die, or if I did not touch the doorknob ten times, I worried I could die. I'd ask my mom the same question over and over, even though she already answered the question. If I touched someone on accident, I would have to tell that person "sorry" three times—otherwise I worried that I could die.

   I don't like my OCD. I knew my OCD was unreasonable, but I didn't know how to stop. I hate my OCD, and I hate how it was trying to control my life! I didn't think anyone could help me. When I first started OCD treatment, I liked it because my doctor helped me get better. He helped me realize that I could fight back against my OCD and that I did not have to listen to what my OCD was telling me. I also realized that I would not die if I didn't do what my OCD told me. My doctor helped me understand I had the power over my life, and I did not have to listen to my OCD and what it told me to do. I learned how to tell my OCD no and learned how to resist the compulsions and rituals.

2. **What motivated you to challenge your OCD?**

   What motivated me to challenge my OCD was that it was making me mentally sick. I was not able to attend school anymore and everyday life was a challenge. I was driving my family crazy, and my anxiety was so high all the time. During treatment, the prizes I could earn each week also helped me to challenge my OCD.

3. **Is there anything you know now about treatment or OCD that you wish you knew before?**

   I wish I knew that I really could get better if I did what my doctor guided me to do. I wish I knew that OCD would not always have control over my life and that I could get better.

4. **Do you have any advice for how family members can best help a child with OCD?**

   I would suggest getting your child ERP. It was a very hard journey to get to where I am today, but it is worth it. Also, I would like to tell family members of a child with OCD that it will be hard on the family during treatment, but once you get through it, your life will be much better.

5. **What advice or words of encouragement do you have for kids who are just starting the process of trying to challenge their OCD?**

   Don't listen to your OCD, it is lying to you! Nothing bad will happen if you don't listen to your OCD.

JULIA, AGE 16

1. **Please share a bit about your experience with OCD.**

   My struggle with OCD began on the day of my fifth birthday. I don't have personal memories of that day, but my mom recalls the following: I had received dresses for my birthday and went to try them on. The dresses were scratchy, and I couldn't get them off fast enough. During this time, my OCD manifested as intense sensory issues. Some mornings before school, it would take me up to two hours to get dressed. None of my clothing felt "right," and I couldn't get past the discomfort. It would take just as much time, several tears, and snacking on Hershey's chocolate bars for me to be able to put my shoes on. My parents brought me to occupational therapy to treat my sensory struggles, but this didn't do much to fight the underlying cause: OCD.

   During fifth grade is when my OCD began to manifest differently. I began to notice that any time I did something that I deemed "morally wrong," I would feel the intense need to confess to my mom. I felt guilty and like I was hiding who I really was from her if I didn't "confess" to her what I had done. I would tell her the same things over and over to make sure she "had the full story." The reassurance that she gave me in those moments fueled my compulsion of reassurance-seeking.

   Around seventh grade, my intrusive thoughts became sexual in nature, which caused a lot of distress for me, and my compulsions intensified. It would bother me if I had an intrusive sexual thought while doing an activity, so my compulsions focused on redoing my actions until I wasn't thinking an intrusive thought while doing them. For example, when I submitted online assignments, I'd try to think of three "neutral" thoughts before an intrusive thought would slip in. This caused me to unsubmit and resubmit assignments over and over until I "got it right." It also caused me to dwell even more on my intrusive thoughts, as I was consciously trying to avoid them.

   I have also struggled with contamination OCD. I would worry about contaminating other people rather than them contaminating me. This caused compulsions such as constant handwashing, sanitizing my phone, and not hanging out with people if I was even slightly sick. By eighth grade, I started medication and talk therapy, but since my therapist wasn't specialized in OCD, it didn't do much to combat my compulsions. It wasn't until I started exposure therapy in tenth grade that my obsessions and compulsions decreased. I strived to be present when I did things, and I did my best to not perform compulsions of thinking neutralizing thoughts. If an intrusive thought slipped in, I would not redo the action. Over time, my intrusive thoughts became much less present.

Being in therapy for OCD has been lifechanging for me. I have learned techniques to stop living in my head and start living in the present moment instead. The level of support and understanding I have received with exposure therapy has been unmatched. Of course, there are still more challenging days, but now I know how I can properly support myself through them. For example, I now clean my phone, at most, once a day (rather than the two times a day I used to), and I try to wash my hands less obsessively. Every day is a journey with OCD, and it has been amazing to learn how to exist alongside it without it taking over my life.

2. **What motivated you to challenge your OCD?**

   I was tired of being stuck in my head all the time. I remembered a time when my thoughts were not all-consuming and I was able to be more present. I knew that this could be my reality again, so I chased it.

3. **Is there anything you know now about treatment or OCD that you wish you knew before?**

   I wish I knew that generic talk therapy was not going to be effective enough to combat my OCD. While it was a great way to get out my feelings, it was not what I needed in terms of exposure therapy and acknowledging my OCD for what it was. I couldn't have imagined how helpful exposure therapy has been.

4. **Do you have any advice for how family members can best help a child with OCD?**

   I want to say that I know it can be hard to see your child struggle and feel like you can't do anything, but there are ways you can help. First, don't create a stigma around OCD, and don't make your child feel like it's something to be ashamed of. If you have the opportunity to get them into therapy (OCD specialized, if possible), I highly recommend doing so, as it can be lifechanging. I have always been accepting of my need to go to therapy to treat my OCD. I owe much of that to my parents and the lack of stigma that they placed on the disorder. I never felt like I had to hide the fact that I have OCD.

   Also, if you begin to notice a pattern of reassurance-seeking, like repeatedly telling your child that they are "not a bad person," know that this may be feeding their OCD and causing them to repeat the compulsion. I suggest asking your child's therapist what the best way to respond is if they are constantly seeking reassurance from you.

5. **What advice or words of encouragement do you have for kids who are just starting the process of trying to challenge their OCD?**

   If you are starting the process of trying to challenge your OCD, I am so proud of you. Having the courage to stand up to something as challenging as OCD shows your immense strength. I also want you to try to give yourself the same grace as you would a best friend or family member you love dearly. Don't be so hard on yourself if the process feels challenging; OCD absolutely *can* be difficult to battle, but standing up to it is so rewarding! Also, know that there will still be hard days and that OCD will creep up on you, no matter how good you feel. That does not mean that you are starting over from square one. In fact, I think those days are a nice reminder that you can persevere and use the techniques you've learned to make your OCD a little less daunting!

HALE, AGE 12

1. **Please share a bit about your experience with OCD.**

   I'd say my OCD started around kindergarten. My OCD is mostly about correction and that "just-right" feeling. For example, if another student said something incorrectly (like them being wrong about something I know a lot about), it would trigger me so much, and I would jump to correct them. In those moments, my OCD was telling me that the other student might get a bad grade or get made fun of for not knowing something, so it was my responsibility to correct them. Unfortunately, the other person would usually react in negative ways even though I was just trying to help them.

   I also have a fear of the germs on handrails, especially those used by little kids who pick their noses or put their hands in their mouths. I'm worried about getting sick, and the thought of touching those germs is gross to me. At my school, there is a stairwell to my classroom upstairs, but it's right by the youngest classes, and I would avoid using it. My OCD is sneaky. At first, I thought I didn't need to use the handrail, or just didn't feel like it, but after working with my OCD therapist, I realized I was avoiding using this particular handrail because of fears about contamination from little kids and their germs. In treatment, I practiced intentionally touching the handrail until my anxious thoughts started to dissipate. I still hesitate to touch it sometimes, but I know pushing past the hesitation is what keeps my OCD in check.

   My OCD also wants me to believe that I'll get unpleasant tastes stuck in my mouth when I eat new foods that I might dislike. My mom has suggested I try thinking about the taste of foods I love if this happens, but I'm afraid the bad taste will contaminate the good tastes and I won't be able to enjoy those foods anymore. (I also learned that any effort to "counter" my OCD worry in this way would have actually been a ritual too.) It is really challenging for me to talk about trying foods that are similar to things I already like, so even thinking about trying other foods takes a lot of effort. I haven't tackled all of my food-related OCD yet, but I know I have the tools and support to make progress when I am ready to.

   In the beginning, it felt like OCD was a curse I was born with. I felt like an outcast because no one else at my school had it (that I knew of) and I didn't feel like I could relate to other people. During my treatment, there were times it felt pointless, like it wasn't doing anything. But the amount of ERP exercises I did (and there were a *lot*!) helped little by little. Looking back, I have come so far. I'm eating foods I've never eaten before, I've touched handrails I used to avoid, and even though it's really hard (and sometimes it still gets me), my teachers say I'm correcting a lot less this year.

2. **What motivated you to challenge your OCD?**

   I started having intrusive thoughts that felt scary while in class, so I talked to my teacher and principal about the thoughts. Even though I was still worried, I felt supported to have so many people I could talk to. Soon after that, I joined a study on OCD where I learned about ERP, and I met with a therapist who taught me about talking back to my OCD.

3. **Is there anything you know now about treatment or OCD that you wish you knew before?**

   Everything! I didn't even know it was OCD in the beginning or anyone else who had it. Now I know those intrusive thoughts are not dangerous, even though they can feel like it. They're like gnats in my mind, and I don't need to worry about them. I'm going to be okay and so are you.

4. **Do you have any advice for how family members can best help a child with OCD?**

   Ask your child if their OCD is making them have intrusive thoughts, because talking about it helps. Push them a little bit at a time when they are having difficult moments with OCD because they might be able to handle a little bit more. Ask for help when your child needs it; my mom got a therapist who understands OCD, and that helped us both figure out how to talk back to my OCD so that things aren't as difficult anymore.

5. **What advice or words of encouragement do you have for kids who are just starting the process of trying to challenge their OCD?**

   OCD doesn't have to be such a scary thing because it's pretty much just your brain playing tricks on you. You have control over your brain, so you have power over your OCD. Also, name your OCD something dumb and cringey because that helps too. Mine is named "Barf."

ASHER, AGE 10

1. **Please share a bit about your experience with OCD.**

   I started to get OCD worries near the beginning of fourth grade. I worried about everything I thought I did wrong (even if they were little things I didn't need to worry about) and would confess all these things to my parents. For example, if I did something where I thought I was mean to someone, I would feel terrible about it until I told a parent—even if the other person didn't care. Or if I thought of something "bad" that happened years ago, I felt the need to tell a parent.

   My OCD would also tell me to wipe the floor clean after using the bathroom, or I would feel bad for not being clean. When I was in the shower, I would have to wash things twice because I'd be unsure if I cleaned myself well. Things like this have bothered me so much and have been a waste of time. Over the past few months, I've gotten a lot better—more than I thought I could have. I had to tell myself to leave the thoughts alone, and they're no big deal.

2. **What motivated you to challenge your OCD?**

   I was having a real hard time. I knew I couldn't keep living like I was, and I wanted to do whatever it took to get rid of my OCD. It was a big downer on my life. It made me feel sad and enjoy things less. That's why I needed to get rid of OCD.

3. **Is there anything you know now about treatment or OCD that you wish you knew before?**

   It is not as hard as you think. You just need to fight back, and little by little, it will go away. I was really surprised by the results I got and how fast it could go away. It was like I had to get over a big hump at the beginning and then it got easier to challenge my OCD. And now it is almost gone.

4. **Do you have any advice for how family members can best help a child with OCD?**

   I think the family needs to work together to keep everyone happy. OCD thoughts can make kids sad or down on themselves. I think parents need to do their best to not get mad and to listen to their child. Let them know that the parent is not upset at the child because of their thoughts. I received a lot of support from my mother and father, which helped a lot.

5. **What advice or words of encouragement do you have for kids who are just starting the process of trying to challenge their OCD?**

   You will get over your OCD. Stay positive. You should know that it is your own mind playing tricks on you. But you can beat it! If you can stay happy and not let the thoughts bother you, you will be great! You can do it!

CHASE, AGE 17

1. **Please share a bit about your experience with OCD.**

   At age twelve, I was at the grocery store with my aunt when I felt an overwhelming amount of anxiety out of the blue. I didn't know how to put into words what I was feeling, so I didn't tell anyone. Eventually, I got home and tried explaining it to my mom, but it was hard. From then on, I woke up every day that summer with obsessive thoughts that I didn't know how to handle—thoughts like "Am I real? How do I know that this isn't just a simulation? What is the purpose of life?" These thoughts consumed my mind for hours and hours on end. No matter where I was, I would be thinking these existential thoughts.

   My compulsions consisted of researching the purpose of life, asking my family if they were real, and trying to understand things that don't have a definite explanation. It got to the point where I couldn't even look at the stars at night because it would cause me to question my existence. Sleep was my only escape, even though I hardly got any sleep due to my constant obsessions. I dreaded waking up in the morning because I knew it would be another day full of obsessions, anxiety, and feeling awful.

   Initially, I thought I was dealing with general anxiety. I didn't know what OCD was at the time. I was one of those people who thought OCD was where you liked being organized. I started seeing a general therapist who helps patients that deal with anxiety, and although it helped a little, the obsessions didn't stop. Eventually, I researched all my symptoms and stumbled across an article explaining "existential OCD." Everything I read in that article explained exactly how I felt and what I was dealing with. I decided to start seeing an OCD therapist, and that changed everything. Through the use of exposure therapy, my obsessions lessened day by day, and I stopped doing compulsions. Although therapy felt scary at first, it has made a world of a difference.

2. **What motivated you to challenge your OCD?**

   Once I learned that challenging my OCD and not giving into my obsessions could help me get better, I was ready to make a change in my thinking. It was tough, but I started exposing myself to things that would make me anxious while not performing any compulsions. Over time, I would get less and less anxious, and exposures would become easier.

3. **Is there anything you know now about treatment or OCD that you wish you knew before?**

   At the start of treatment, I wish I knew that it was going to be hard but very worth it. I used to think that my OCD was going to haunt me for my whole life and that therapy wouldn't help that much, but I was very wrong.

4. **Do you have any advice for how family members can best help a child with OCD?**

   Some advice I would give to family members of a person with OCD is to stop reassuring them. Reassurance is something that people with OCD seek to make them feel better, but in reality, it does more harm than good. To improve, you have to be able to sit with your OCD, not have reassurance, and just accept the presence of your thoughts.

5. **What advice or words of encouragement do you have for kids who are just starting the process of trying to challenge their OCD?**

   Just trust the process! Allow your thoughts to be there but don't fight them. Although it may seem impossible, with the right tools, you can beat your OCD! Expose yourself to things that make you anxious without performing any compulsions. At first, you may think it's too hard and not worth it, but over time it is definitely worth it. So, just trust the process.

All of these real kids decided to share their experiences with OCD to help you see that you are not alone and that you can get better too (even if you have doubts)! Hopefully, their stories helped you see that it is worth it to put in the work to overcome OCD.

The next chapter concludes this workbook by reviewing some extra words of motivation to help you feel empowered in your journey to gain control over OCD!

CHAPTER 15

Additional Motivation to Inspire You!

Wow! You made it! As we reach this final chapter, take a moment to recognize all that you have learned. Hopefully, you now feel more prepared and ready to gain control over your *tricky, sticky, picky* brain. Maybe you're excited. Maybe you're worried. Perhaps you're both. However you feel right now is okay, as the most important thing you can do to conquer OCD is to start somewhere and take action—one step at a time. Keep going and don't give up. It's worth it to get to the other side.

I've learned that kids with OCD are some of the strongest kids in the world. That's because when you have a *tricky, sticky, picky* brain, your OCD commands you to do what it wants—and treatment basically requires doing the *opposite* of that. Think about how big of a deal that is! How many other things in life are like that?! So, if you can do this, there isn't anything you can't do.

I put together the following words of inspiration to help me on my own journey against OCD, and I am excited to share them with you. I hope the extra encouragement can motivate you as well. You can do it, just like I did!

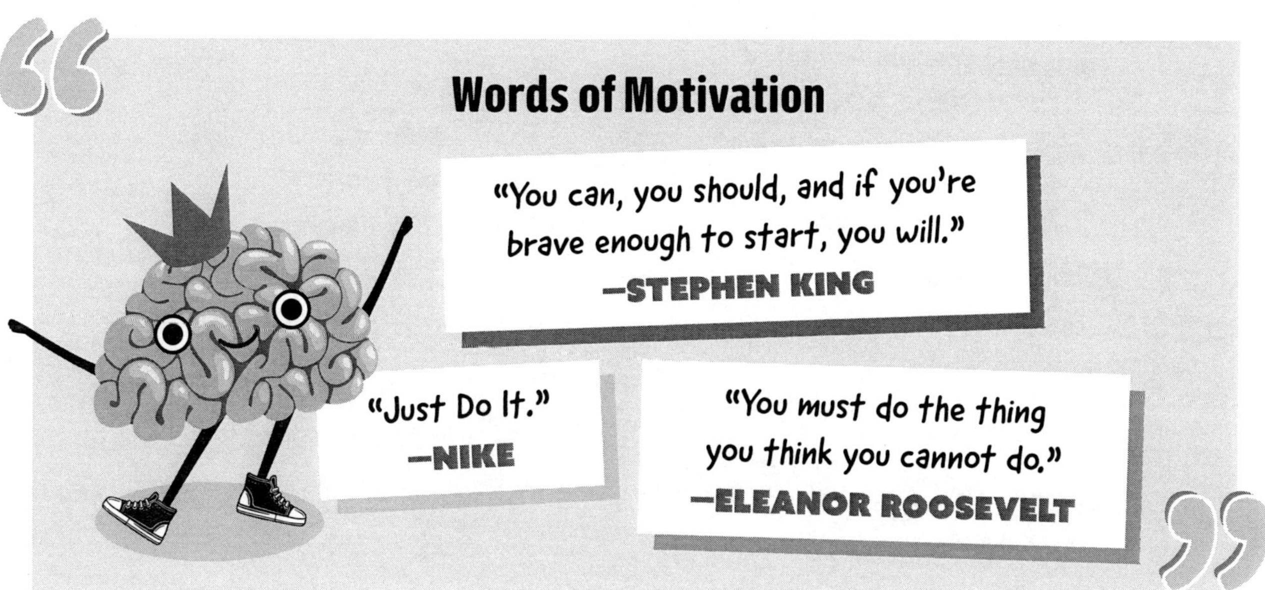

"Don't underestimate what you can accomplish by taking small steps."

"A champion is defined not by their wins, but by how they can recover when they fall."
—SERENA WILLIAMS

"Never confuse a single defeat with a final defeat."
—F. SCOTT FITZGERALD

"You can't stop the waves, but you can learn to surf."
—JON KABAT-ZINN

"Be stronger than your excuses."
—ERIC THOMAS

"The best way out is always through."
—ROBERT FROST

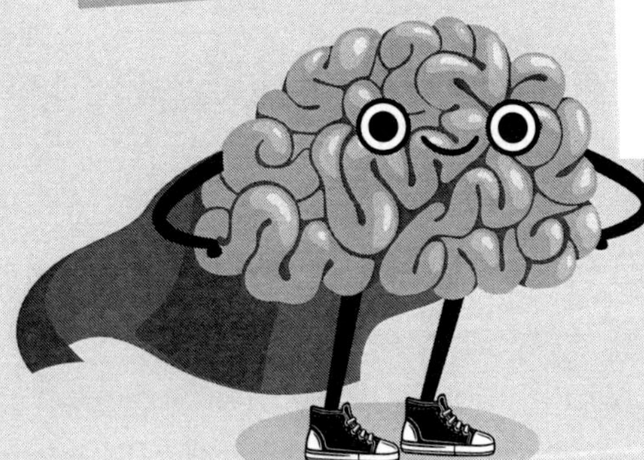

"Confront your fears and they won't be your fears anymore."

"Progress, not perfection."

"You miss 100 percent of the shots you don't take."
—WAYNE GRETZKY

"Even the darkest night will end and the sun will rise."
—VICTOR HUGO

"Today is a good day to do tough things."

"You've survived 100 percent of your worst days. Keep going."

"Feel the fear and do it anyway."
—SUSAN JEFFERS

"You are stronger than you think."

"If you don't make the time to work on creating the life you want, you're eventually going to be forced to spend a lot of time dealing with a life you don't want."
—KEVIN NGO

"You get what you work for, not what you wish for."
—DANIEL MILSTEIN

"The man who moves a mountain begins by carrying away small stones."
—CONFUCIUS

"Obstacles don't have to stop you. If you run into a wall, don't turn around and give up. Figure out how to climb it, go through it, or work around it."
—MICHAEL JORDAN

"Start where you are. Use what you have. Do what you can."
—ARTHUR ASHE

"It always seems impossible until it's done."
—NELSON MANDELA

"Do not let what you cannot do interfere with what you can do."
—JOHN WOODEN

"A year from now you may wish you had started today."
—KAREN LAMB

"Where there is a will, there is a way."

"Do not wait; the time will never be 'just right.' Start where you stand, and work with whatever tools you may have at your command, and better tools will be found as you go along."
—NAPOLEON HILL

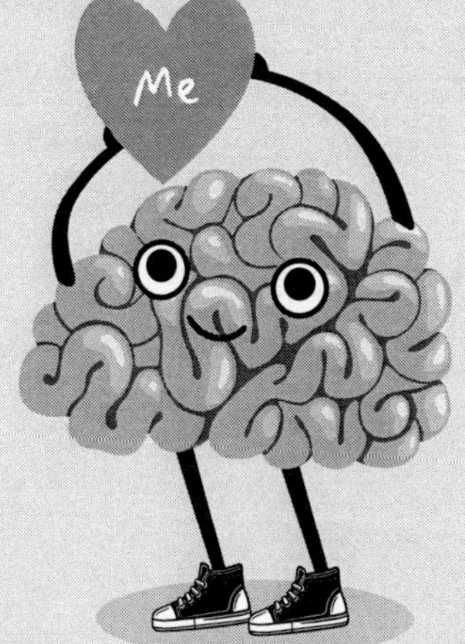

"Most of the important things in the world have been accomplished by people who have kept on trying when there seemed to be no hope at all."
—DALE CARNEGIE

"Do what you can, with what you have, where you are."
—THEODORE ROOSEVELT

"Change will not come if we wait for some other person, or if we wait for some other time. We are the ones we've been waiting for. We are the change that we seek."
—BARACK OBAMA

"Do something today that your future self will thank you for."
—SEAN PATRICK FLANERY

"We should not let our fears hold us back from pursuing our hopes."
—JOHN F. KENNEDY

"It doesn't matter where you are coming from. All that matters is where you are going."
—BRIAN TRACY

"Taking a step backward after taking a step forward is not a disaster, it's a cha-cha."
—ROBERT BRAULT

"There are no shortcuts to any place worth going."
—BEVERLY SILLS

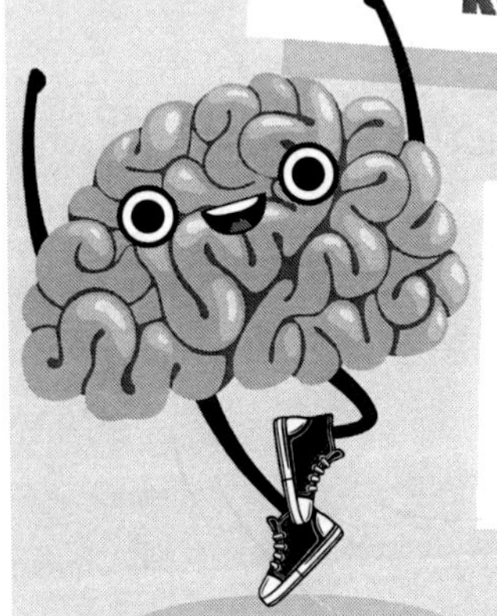

"Sometimes the smallest step in the right direction ends up being the biggest step of your life. Tip toe if you must, but take the step."
—NAEEM CALLAWAY

Acknowledgments

To all the children, parents, and families I have worked with over the years—it has genuinely been an honor to be a part of your journey. It is my work with patients that has helped refine my skills so that I could ultimately share them with a larger audience through this book. Thank you for putting your trust in me.

To my family, thank you for all of your love, support, and encouragement over the years. Especially to my mother, Karen—you are a strong and amazing woman, and I am lucky to have you as my mom.

To all my mentors, colleagues, and friends—I am extremely grateful for the relationships we have built over the years, as well as the ongoing learning I achieve through having you all in my life. I am also grateful to those of you who provided feedback as I put this book together. Particular thanks to Eric Storch, whose mentorship has been invaluable in my growth as a clinician and professional. Your insights have shaped so much of my work, and I am incredibly grateful for your constant support and encouragement.

To the *real kids* who contributed to this book—thank you for turning your pain into a purpose by sharing your stories. You should be proud of yourself, as I know that your vulnerability will help others. I'd also like to thank my team at the Jacob Center for Evidence-Based Treatment. It is a privilege to work with you and be a part of the quality care that you provide to our community.

To Kayla Church, Jenessa Jackson, and the staff at PESI Publishing—thank you for your support, guidance, and enthusiasm in bringing this project together. It has been a pleasure to work with you all. I especially appreciate your willingness to let me pack so much into this book with the goal that it could help as many people as possible.

To the International OCD Foundation—you are an incredible community that I am grateful to be a part of. Thank you for your mission and the amazing work that you do to bring resources to those who suffer with this tough but treatable disorder.

To all the children, adolescents, parents, and family members who read this book—I hope it helps you on your journey. Just remember, OCD doesn't have to stop you from anything.

About the Author

Marni L. Jacob, PhD, ABPP, is a licensed psychologist and clinical director of the Jacob Center for Evidence-Based Treatment in Boca Raton, Florida, which specializes in the treatment of obsessive-compulsive disorder (OCD), obsessive-compulsive spectrum disorders, anxiety disorders, and phobias in children, adolescents, and adults. Dr. Jacob is board certified in clinical child and adolescent psychology, and she has published over 45 peer-reviewed journal articles and book chapters. Dr. Jacob is actively involved as a leader in the psychology community, previously serving as president of the nonprofit organization OCD Central & South Florida (a regional affiliate of the International OCD Foundation), and president of the Palm Chapter of the Florida Psychological Association. She is a strong proponent of the dissemination of evidence-based treatment, frequently presents on OCD, anxiety, and related disorders at national conferences, and also trains clinicians by serving as a faculty member of the International OCD Foundation's (IOCDF) Pediatric Behavior Therapy Training Institute (BTTI).